American Book Company's

PASSING THE
WRITING
GRADUATION TEST
IN
GEORGIA

ALIGNED TO THE NEW DOMAINS
AND THE GPS STANDARDS

DEVIN PINTOZZI,
MARIA STRUDER, and BRIAN FREEL

AMERICAN BOOK COMPANY
PO BOX 2638
WOODSTOCK, GEORGIA 30188-1383
TOLL-FREE PHONE: 1-888-264-5877   TOLL-FREE FAX: 1-866-827-3240
WEB SITE: www.americanbookcompany.com

C0-AUG-501

ACKNOWLEDGEMENTS

The authors are grateful to Kelly Berg for her help in formatting and developing graphics for this book. We also want to thank the many students and teachers whose needs and suggestions have guided us in preparing this book. Special thanks go to Margaret DuPree and Zuzana Urbanek for revisions to the 2007 edition.

Excerpt on page 53 is adapted from Allison Sloan's "How Consumers Impact Biodiversity," copyright © 2000. Reprinted from *The Green Guide* (#79) with permission from Mothers & Others for a Livable Planet.

This product/publication includes images from CorelDRAW 9 which are protected by the copyright laws of the United States, Canada, and elsewhere. Used under license.

Copyright ©2007
by American Book Company
PO Box 2638
Woodstock, GA 30188-1383

ALL RIGHTS RESERVED

The text of this publication, or any part thereof, may not be reproduced or transmitted in any form or by any means, electronic or mechanical, including photocopying, recording, storage in an information retrieval system, or otherwise, without the prior permission of the publisher.

Printed in the United States of America

03/01   04/04   08/07

Table of Contents

PREFACE iv

**PREPARING FOR THE GEORGIA
HIGH SCHOOL WRITING TEST** v

DIAGNOSTIC ESSAY 1
What to Expect 1
Diagnostic Essay 6
Evaluating the Diagnostic Essay 12
Sample Diagnostic Essay 13

WRITING EVALUATION CHART 14

CHAPTER 1 15
Writing Paragraphs
Paragraph Structure 15
Writing a Topic Sentence 18
Improving a Topic Sentence 19
Supporting Details 22
Developing Supporting Details 24
Organizing Paragraphs 26
Writing a Concluding Sentence 30
Chapter 1 Summary 32
Chapter 1 Review 33
Additional Activities 36

CHAPTER 2 37
Writing to Persuade
Author's Purpose 37
Audience 40
Language and Tone 43
Using Persuasive Language 46
Building an Argument 48
Chapter 2 Summary 56
Chapter 2 Review 57
Additional Activities 60

CHAPTER 3 61
Planning the Essay
Basic Structure of an Essay 61
The Writing Process 62
Read the Writing Prompt Carefully 63
Generating Ideas 64
Focusing Ideas 66
Making a Plan 69
Chapter 3 Summary 71
Chapter 3 Review 72
Additional Activities 76

CHAPTER 4 77
Drafting the Essay
Improving Word Choice 77
Choosing Active Voice 81
Writing Introductions 83

Writing Conclusions 87
Using Transitional Words 89
Developing Coherence 95
Writing the Draft 97
Chapter 4 Summary 99
Chapter 4 Review 100
Additional Activities 101

CHAPTER 5 102
Revising the Essay
How to Revise 102
Adding Clarifying Information 104
Deleting Unrelated Sentences 105
Eliminating Unnecessary Words 107
Correcting Shifts in Tense or Person 109
Checking for Parallel Sentence Structure 112
Developing Sentence Variety 114
Chapter 5 Summary 117
Chapter 5 Review 118
Additional Activities 120

CHAPTER 6 122
Proofreading the Essay
Proofreading Notation 122
Capitalization 123
Internal Punctuation 124
Grammar and Usage 129
Spelling 140
Sentence Formation 143
Chapter 6 Summary 148
Chapter 6 Review 149
Additional Activities 152

CHAPTER 7 153
Scoring the Essay
Scoring Overview 153
    Requirements 154
    Domains 154
    Five-Point Scale 155
    Analytic and Holistic Grading 155
Ideas 156
Organization 160
Style 163
Conventions 167
Chapter 7 Summary 171
Chapter 7 Review 172
Additional Activities 175

APPENDIX A 177
Additional Writing Prompts

APPENDIX B 185
Writing Resources

Preface

About the Book

Passing the Writing Graduation Test in Georgia provides students with instruction and practice for Georgia's High School Writing Test. **This edition has been revised to align with the new domains and the Georgia Performance Standards (GPS) for the high school writing assessment.** This book will benefit students who are preparing to take the writing test for the first time or those preparing for a retest. Students will learn the basics of planning, drafting, revising, and editing an essay, with primary emphasis on persuasive writing. We recommend that students keep a portfolio of their writing so they can see their skills progress over time.

After each lesson, practice exercises help students master the concepts that they learned in the lesson. Individual and group activities provide opportunities for further practice for students in classes or in individualized study sessions. Students and teachers can rehearse the test situation by responding to the list of sample writing prompts in Appendix A. Appendix B contains lists of books and Web sites that may also help students develop their writing skills. The separate teacher's answer key also contains a chart of standards.

For students who may need more review of grammar and usage skills, American Book Company offers a companion book, *Basics Made Easy: Grammar and Usage Review*, with accompanying software.

We welcome comments and suggestions about this book. Please contact:

Zuzana Urbanek, English/Language Arts Curriculum Coordinator

American Book Company
PO Box 2638
Woodstock, GA 30188-1383

Toll Free: 1 (888) 264-5877
Phone: (770) 928-2834
Fax: (770) 928-7483

Web site: www.americanbookcompany.com

About the Authors

Devin Pintozzi is a graduate of Oglethorpe University in Atlanta, Georgia where he majored in psychology and minored in history. He is a full-time writer who strives for clear and concise communication in his publications. Recently, he earned an MBA from Georgia State University.

Maria Struder graduated from Kennesaw State University, Kennesaw, Georgia, with a Bachelor of Arts in English. She has taught writing skills at the college level and home schooled her two children. She is now a writer and editor, specializing in English Language Arts.

Brian Freel holds a Bachelor of Arts degree from Amherst College in Amherst, Massachusetts, and a Master of Arts degree from St. Mary's University in Baltimore, Maryland. He is a writer specializing in language arts and history. He has taught students at middle school, high school, and adult levels.

American Book Company has produced best-selling books on passing end of course and exit exams in Alabama, Arizona, California, Florida, Georgia, Indiana, Louisiana, Maryland, Minnesota, Nevada, New Jersey, North Carolina, Ohio, South Carolina, Tennessee, and Texas.

Preparing for the Georgia High School Writing Test

Students who entered grade nine after July 1, 1994, must pass the Georgia High School Writing Test as one requirement for earning a high school diploma. This test is one of five exams now required for graduation from Georgia high schools. The other tests are in English language arts, mathematics, science, and social studies.

What is the Georgia High School Writing Test (GHSWT)?

This test requires students to write a persuasive essay in response to a writing prompt.

What is a persuasive essay?

An essay is a relatively brief piece of writing focused on one topic. For the purpose of this test, an essay is considered to be a composition of three to five paragraphs. In persuasive writing, the author chooses one side of an issue and tries to convince the reader to agree with that position. The author may use a variety of forms while writing persuasively. For example, an author may narrate a story which shows his or her position on a particular issue.

When do I take the GHSWT?

You will be tested in the fall of your junior year.

How much time do I have to take the test?

The total testing time is two hours. Of that time, 100 minutes is for student writing. The remainder of the time is for handing out tests, filling out the information sheet, etc.

How long does my essay have to be?

There is no length requirement, except that your paper must be a well-developed essay. In the Ideas domain, raters look at both the depth of development and the fluency (amount) of development. A paper that consists of only a paragraph or two rarely has enough variety and/or complexity to receive more than a low score. Likewise, filling both pages of the test document does not guarantee a higher score. A two-page paper without a focus and relevant supporting ideas could still receive a score of "1."

Do I need to write the test in cursive?

No. You may either print or write in cursive. If you print, do NOT use all capital letters, as this prevents the proper grading of capitalization.

Can I bring a dictionary with me to use during the writing assessment?

No. Because Conventions (including spelling) is tested, students cannot use dictionaries during the writing test.

How is the GHSWT scored?

Each paper is scored independently by two raters. Raters who score the essays are trained to understand and use the standardized scoring system. Each of the four domains of effective writing is evaluated. Although these domains are interrelated during the writing process, a strength or area of challenge is scored only once under a particular domain. Scores in each domain range from 1 to 5 (5 being the highest score). The combined scores represent a continuum of writing that ranges from inadequate to minimal to good to very good. Points on the continuum are defined by the scoring rubric for each domain. Domain scores are combined to obtain a total score for each student.

Your essay will be graded according to four domains, including:

Ideas	(40%)
Organization	(20%)
Style	(20%)
Conventions	(20%)

The total score is then converted to a three-digit scaled score. There are three performance levels represented: Does Not Meet (100-199), Meets (200-249), and Exceeds (250+).

What kinds of errors count the most against my score?

Basically, the rater's task boils down to three questions in each domain: How much of this is correct? Did the writer attempt anything complex? Does the writer demonstrate variety in the components?

Raters read for competence in each domain, not to tally errors. A writer may demonstrate good skills in a domain even though the paper contains errors in some areas of that domain. Remember that the paper you turn in is essentially a draft, not a polished, ready-to-publish classroom assignment. A rater does not begin with a perfect paper in mind and "knock off" points for errors. A rater examines the essay for what the writer does right. Nearly every student paper contains errors. It is the degree of control, the proportion of correct to incorrect instances, and the complexity of what is attempted that determine the score in each domain.

What happens if I don't pass the writing test?

The test is administered in the fall, spring, and summer. If you fail when you first take the test, you can retest during a future administration of the test before your completion of the 12th grade. If you fail to pass, but you have met all other requirements for graduation, you may be eligible for a Certificate of Attendance. You may attempt the graduation test again, as often as you need to in order to qualify for a high school diploma.

If I fail the writing test, where can I seek help to improve my score the next time?

You can improve your score in several ways. You can continue developing your writing skills in your regular English classes. You can attend special classes or individualized sessions where you work with tutors, other students, or teachers. In addition, you can sign up for special summer classes in your school district.

Diagnostic Essay

The first step in preparing for success on a test is to know what to expect. The second step is to practice the skills necessary to succeed at the task required by the test. In this chapter, you will learn about the format of the Georgia High School Writing Test (GHSWT), take a practice test, and evaluate a sample essay. The essay you produce will show you and your instructor where your strengths are and which writing skills you need to practice more. You can then focus on the chapters in this book that will benefit you the most. This **diagnostic essay** is just the beginning of the journey you will take to improve your writing skills and pass the GHSWT.

WHAT TO EXPECT

When you take the GHSWT, you may bring only pens and pencils. Paper will be provided for you. You may not bring any other books, notes, or papers. You will receive a **test booklet** which includes the following:

1. An **information page** where you write your full name, school, social security number and other relevant personal information. Make sure you remember your social security number.

2. **Test-taking directions** that describe the requirements of the test and provide you with guidelines for how to use your time during the test.

3. A description of the **Writing Situation** and the **Directions for Writing**. These instructions give you the issue you are to address, the type of writing you are to do (a letter, a proposal, etc.), and the audience to whom you will write.

4. A **writing checklist** that gives you brief reminders about how to write an effective essay.

5. **Two pages of planning and prewriting space** for brainstorming, outlining, and a first draft. This part will not be graded. You may ask for additional sheets of paper by raising your hand.

6. **Two pages of lined paper for your final copy**. This is the only writing that will be graded. Make sure your writing is clear and neat. You may print or write in cursive, but you must use a pen.

Writing Situation and Directions for Writing

The GHSWT requires you to respond to a writing prompt. This prompt consists of two parts: the <u>Writing Situation</u> and the <u>Directions for Writing</u>. Look at the sample below. It is a released writing prompt from a previously administered test and will not be used in future tests.

<u>Writing Situation</u>

Health care advancements have resulted in people living longer. Many Americans now live well beyond the age of 65. This older generation consists of people with various experiences, talents, and expertise. Many of these senior citizens have retired from the workforce and can now use their talents in the service of their community. Think of how your community could benefit from the contributions of these older Americans.

<u>Directions for Writing</u>

Write a speech to be given at an organization of senior citizens explaining your ideas. Convince the senior citizens that they should give their services to benefit the community. Provide logical arguments and supporting details.

The GHSWT uses a variety of writing prompts about different issues. Each prompt is worded differently, but each will have the same six elements listed below.

1. Issue

The issue is the topic which you will discuss. It will be relevant to the interests and experiences of high school students. The issue may be related to school, concerns of teens, social problems, or other topics. What is the issue in the prompt above?

2. Descriptive Setup

The writing prompt will provide a brief background to the issue that you are to consider. It will try to put the issue in a realistic context and provide any additional information necessary to discuss the issue. The context may be historical, literary, current, or hypothetical. Underline the descriptive setup in the prompt above.

3. Knowledge Base

The GHSWT does not allow time for you to research the topic given in the writing prompt. You are expected to discuss the issue based on your personal and/or academic experiences. What areas of knowledge could you draw from to discuss the prompt above?

4. Writer's Intent and Writing Task

The writing prompt will ask you to do one of the following: examine different sides of a controversy; choose a position, and provide support for that position; or analyze a problem and its solution(s). To accomplish one of these tasks, you will write a persuasive essay. What is the writer's intent and writing task in the prompt on this page?

Copyright © American Book Company

5. Audience

The writing prompt will describe the audience to whom you will write. It may be someone familiar such as your family or fellow students, or it may be people whom you may not know such as school board members, government officials, or readers of the local newspaper. You will need to take the audience into account as you write your essay. Who is the audience described in the sample prompt?

6. Form

The prompt will also give you a certain form to follow in composing your response. It may be a letter or a speech, a composition or a position paper, or some other form of writing. Your essay will be evaluated on the appropriate use of form, but not on the special conventions of a particular form. For example, you will not be graded on whether you include your address on a letter. Think about what form is required by the sample prompt.

Knowing the key elements of the writing prompt will help you respond to the assigned task, use the appropriate form, and address the proper audience.

How to Use Your Time

The total time for the Writing Test is two hours. Twenty minutes are devoted to the administrative tasks of filling out the information sheet, answering any questions from students, and collecting the test booklets at the conclusion of the test. The other 100 minutes are allotted for student writing. The educators who designed the test recommend that you use the time in the following way:

Planning/Prewriting   (15 minutes)
Read the writing prompt carefully, brainstorm ideas, and organize those ideas in a clustering diagram or outline.

Drafting   (35 minutes)
Once you have organized your ideas, write them in complete sentences developed into well-formed paragraphs. You do not need to worry much about grammar and punctuation at this point.

Revising   (20 minutes)
Now is the time to read over your draft and make improvements. You want to make sure all of your ideas are developed in a logical order and supported by relevant reasons and examples. You also want to eliminate unrelated ideas and unnecessary words. This is a good time to improve your word choice as well. Then, write your final draft on the lined paper.

Final Draft   (20 minutes)
Rewrite your draft on 2 pages of lined paper. When you take the actual Writing Assessment, pages will be provided in the Answer Document.

Proofreading   (10 minutes)
Take advantage of the last few minutes of the testing time to review your essay one more time. This time look for errors in capitalization, punctuation, and grammar. These small corrections can make a big difference.

The times given for each part are only suggestions. You may spend more or less time on any one part. Just remember, you can use all of the 100 minutes for your essay. Use your time wisely.

Requirements

To make sure your paper can be graded properly, you must do the following:

Write on the assigned topic. Make sure you clearly understand the topic, purpose, and audience for your assignment. Keep a clear focus, and do not stray from it.

Write in English. This test is intended to evaluate your skill in writing Standard American English.

Write legibly. You want the graders of your essay to be able to read it easily. You may have great ideas, but if the graders can't read them, you will not get credit for them.

Write a well-developed composition. Though you have only 100 minutes, this is enough time for you to organize your ideas into a three- to five-paragraph essay. Write an introduction, one to three paragraphs of support, and a conclusion.

Write in prose. This is not a test in poetry. Extended use of musical lyrics will not be graded.

Write respectfully. Essays that use offensive language or discuss offensive content may not be graded. If you can't express your ideas without vulgarity, then don't express them.

Write on the two pages of lined paper. Your final draft must fit in this allotted space. The graders will not consider any other writing.

By fulfilling these requirements, you guarantee only that your paper will be graded. In order for your paper to receive a passing grade or an excellent grade, you must follow the criteria outlined in the next section.

Copyright © American Book Company

How Your Paper Will Be Scored

Your paper will be graded on four different categories of writing called **domains**. You will receive a separate score for each domain. These scores will be added together to make your final score. The four domains and their components are listed below.

1. **Ideas (40%)** The degree to which the writer establishes a controlling idea and elaborates the main points with examples, illustrations, facts, or details that are appropriate to the persuasive genre. This domain includes the following components:

   Controlling idea/focus   Depth of development
   Supporting ideas   Awareness of the persuasive purpose
   Relevance of detail   Sense of completeness

2. **Organization (20%)** The degree to which the writer's ideas are arranged in a clear order and the overall structure of the response is consistent with the persuasive genre. This domain includes the following components:

   Overall plan   Grouping ideas within paragraphs
   Introduction/body/conclusion   Organizing strategies appropriate to persuasion
   Sequence of ideas   Transitions

3. **Style (20%)** The degree to which the writer demonstrates control of sentence formation, usage, and mechanics. Note: In general, sentence formation and usage are weighted more heavily than mechanics in determining the overall conventions score. This domain includes the following components:

   Word choice   Voice
   Audience awareness   Sentence variety

4. **Conventions (20%)** The writer forms sentences correctly. This domain includes the following elements:

   Sentence formation: correctness, clarity of meaning, complexity, end punctuation
   Usage: subject-verb agreement, standard word forms, verb tenses
   Mechanics: internal punctuation, spelling, paragraph breaks, capitalization

    If, for some reason, the grader is unable to give you a score for each domain, your paper will not pass. For example, if your paper is illegible or not written in English, the grader cannot give you a score. If you paper is off topic, your paper cannot be graded in the Ideas domain. Even if you do well in the other domains, you cannot achieve an overall passing score.

    Later chapters in this book will discuss the skills and strategies you need to score well in each of the four domains.

DIAGNOSTIC ESSAY

You have had an overall introduction to the GHSWT, and now you are familiar with the different parts of the test. You know what to expect. Now it is time to practice the testing situation by completing a diagnostic essay. The next few pages are designed to be very similar to the Georgia High School Writing Test. Use the lined paper on pages 8 to 11 for your draft and final copy. Your instructor will tell you when to begin and when the 100-minute testing time is complete. Do your best, and remember, this is just your first attempt. As you study the chapters in this book, you will have more time for improvement.

Writing Prompt

<u>Writing Situation</u>

In the past, schools hired their own cafeteria staff to provide nutritious, home-cooked student lunches at a low price. Today, private food service companies are claiming that they can provide better school lunches at lower prices. Your local school board is considering a proposal which would allow several food service companies to set up operation in the school cafeteria. Some parents are concerned that students will eat nothing but "fast food." Decide what you think about private companies providing school lunches.

<u>Directions for Writing</u>

Write a letter to the school board that clearly expresses your position on private companies providing school lunches. Try to convince the board members to agree with you by using well-developed arguments.

Writing Checklist

Prepare Yourself to Write
    Read the topic carefully
    Understand the purpose
    Identify the audience

Make Your Paper Meaningful
    State a clearly developed position
    Use specific, convincing, and
        interesting details
    Present ideas in a clear order

Make Your Paper Interesting to Read
    Use effective word choice
    Vary the sentence type, structure, and
        length
    Use convincing and appealing
        supporting details

Make Your Paper Easy to Read
    Write effective paragraphs
    Use effective transitions
    Write in complete and correct sentences
    Capitalize, spell, and punctuate correctly
    Write legibly

Copyright © American Book Company

Directions

This test is to find out how well you write prose on a given topic in the time and space allowed. The test has four time periods or parts. Read the directions for each of these four parts carefully. The times given for each part are recommendations, not rules; if you finish any of the parts early, you may go on to the next part. You have two pages of lined paper for your planning and draft and two pages for your final draft of this diagnostic test. Keep in mind, as you plan and write, that your final copy must fit on two pages. Your paper will be read by persons like your teachers and scored on how well you express your ideas.

In order for your paper to be properly scored, it is very important that you write on the given topic and in prose. Papers that consist entirely or mostly of poetry, musical lyrics, or rap will not be scored. Additionally, papers which are offensive in language or content may not be scored.

Part 1: Plan/Prewrite (15 minutes)

Read your assigned topic on the <u>Writing Prompt</u> page. Review the Writing Checklist to make sure you cover each of the points listed. Use your own paper for planning and prewriting, including making your notes, brainstorming list, or outline.

Part 2: Draft Your Essay (35 minutes)

Using your notes, brainstorming list, or outline, write a first draft of your paper on pages 8 and 9. Don't worry too much about grammar and punctuation at this point. Concentrate on getting your ideas down on paper in logical order.

Part 3: Revise and Edit (20 minutes)

Reread what you have written. Ask yourself if your ideas are clearly and completely expressed. Consider rearranging your ideas and changing words to make your paper better.

Part 4: Write the Final Draft (20 minutes)

Rewrite your paper on pages 10 and 11. When you rewrite, make sure that you use a pen and that you write neatly. You may either print or write in cursive. Do not use any other pages of this section for your writing, and do not write in the margins.

Part 5: Proofread (10 minutes)

When you finish writing your paper, review the points on the <u>Writing Checklist</u> and make any needed corrections in your paper, such as adding punctuation and correcting spelling. You may strike through words, but do so neatly.

DRAFT

Copyright © American Book Company

Copyright © American Book Company

FINAL COPY

SAMPLE DIAGNOSTIC ESSAY

Opening of Letter → Dear Members of the School Board:

Introduction →

Controlling Idea →

What did you have for lunch today? I don't mean to be too personal, but I'll bet you had a choice of just about anything you wanted to eat. Your lunch situation would be very different if you ate in our school cafeteria where there are very few choices. You are considering a proposal which would allow several food service companies to set up operation in the school cafeteria. **I believe you should support this proposal because the competition between companies will produce a greater variety of menu items, higher quality food, and increased portions for the same price.**

Topic Sentence →

First Body Paragraph →

First of all, allowing private companies to serve food in the school cafeteria will increase the variety of meals available. Under the current system, if a student does not want the one meal offered, that student must either run to the vending machines for junk food or go hungry. On the other hand, if there are several companies in the cafeteria offering various choices, every student will be able to find a good lunch to eat. As you can see having several food companies in the cafeteria will decrease the number of students who eat junk food.

Topic Sentence →

Second Body Paragraph →

Second, bringing more than one food provider into the cafeteria will increase the overall quality of the food offered. When one company enjoys a monopoly, it can offer low quality products. However, if several companies are competing for our dollars, they will try their hardest to make their food items as delicious as possible. They know that if the items are not tasty, students can get in a different line. This competition will improve the quality of our food more than any other.

Topic Sentence →

Third Body Paragraph →

Third, having several food providers will allow us to get more food for the same amount of money. Food quality is important to teens, but so is quantity. A growing teenager can't live on standard F.D.A. portions. We need larger meals to fuel our developing minds and bodies. For this reason, student will try to get the most food for their money. Therefore, companies will increase the amount of food they put on each plate in the hopes that students will choose them when they enter the cafeteria. I guarantee you, the company which offers the most food will be very popular with the jocks.

Conclusion →

Summary of Key Ideas →

Some parents are concerned that private companies will give us only junk food to eat. However, as the meals are now in the cafeteria, many students choose hunger or vending machines over the school lunches. Surely a private company can provide a better meal than that. **In fact, competition between several companies will improve the variety, quality, and quantity of food offered for the same low price.** I urge the board to adopt the Resolution and begin seeking bids from food providers in our area.

Closing of Letter →

Sincerely,
Jelisa H. Wilson

Copyright © American Book Company

EVALUATING THE DIAGNOSTIC ESSAY

The sample essay on the facing page responds to the diagnostic writing prompt. Read the essay, and compare it with yours. The read the analysis below.

Analysis of Sample Essay

This sample essay is strong in all four domains evaluated by the GHSWT. The writer clearly states the controlling idea (Ideas), develops relevant support in a logical order (Organization), and uses appropriate tone and word choice (Style). Although there are some errors in mechanics and usage, overall the writer has a good command of standard written English and uses a varied and complex sentence structure (Conventions). Read the more detailed analysis below:

Form: The writer appropriately addresses the letter to the members of the local school board and signs the letter at the end. Though graders will not evaluate the special conventions of a particular form, for example, putting a colon after the opening in a business letter, addressing the letter to the school board shows that the writer understands the writing task, is aware of the audience, and uses the proper form.

Introduction: The introduction begins with a question. This is one good way to catch the reader's interest. The writer then focuses that interest on the topic of the essay. The controlling idea is clearly stated in the last sentence of the introduction. The three points of the controlling idea provide the order for the following body paragraphs.

First Body Paragraph: The writer shows a logical development of ideas by using the first point of the controlling idea as the topic sentence of the first body paragraph. The writer uses a compare and contrast method of argument, describing the current situation in the cafeteria, and then showing how the private companies will make the situation better. The argument is strengthened by trying to address the concerns of parents regarding junk food. The last sentence is missing a comma after "As you can see."

Second Body Paragraph: The second body paragraph uses the second point of the controlling idea for the topic sentence and, again, supports this idea through a comparison and contrast. In the last sentence, "more than any other" has no clear reference and should be eliminated.

Third Body Paragraph: The third body paragraph shows the logic and coherence of the essay by continuing to develop the controlling idea. The fifth sentence should read "student**s** will try . . ." In the sixth sentence, it is unclear whether "them" refers to students or to the companies. The use of the word "jocks" in the last sentence is inappropriate for a letter to the school board. "Athletes" is a better word.

Conclusion: The conclusion addresses the opposition to the writer's position. This approach shows that the writer has thought about the different sides of the issue, giving more credibility to the writer's reasons. The writer includes a brief summary, not a restatement, of the controlling idea. The last sentence encourages the board to take action. This is a good way to end a persuasive essay. The word "resolution" does not need to be capitalized.

Writing Evaluation Chart

The chapters in this book will provide you with several opportunities to practice writing essays. In addition, you will find thirty sample writing prompts in **Appendix A**. Keep all of your essays in one folder. As you prepare for the Georgia High School Writing Test by writing practice essays, you can use the **Writing Evaluation Chart** below to help you assess your progress.

For each essay, work with your teacher or tutor to give yourself a grade in each category listed. If you have an excellent grasp of the skill, write **E** for **Excellent**. If you use the skill well enough to pass, write **P** for **Passing**. If you need to practice a skill more in order to master it, write **NP** for **Needs Practice**. The number listed next to each skill indicates the chapter which discusses that skill. Read and review the chapters you need to improve each skill.

Writing Evaluation Chart

Writing Skills	*Chapter Number*	Diagnostic	1	2	3	4	5	6	7	8	9	10
Effective Topic Sentences	1											
Relevant Supporting Details	1											
Sense of Tone and Audience	2											
Persuasive Argument	2											
Generating and Organizing Ideas	3											
Transitions and Coherence	4											
Effective Word Choice	4											
Sentence Variety	5											
Clear and Concise Words or Ideas	5											
Standard Grammar	6											
Proper Punctuation	6											
Correct Spelling	6											

Copyright © American Book Company

Chapter 1
Writing Paragraphs

The Georgia High School Writing Test (GHSWT) requires you to produce an essay on an assigned topic within a specified amount of time. Each chapter in this book will help you with different aspects of this task. You will begin by writing well-organized paragraphs because any well-written essay is composed of effective paragraphs. In this chapter, you will learn about the following aspects of writing paragraphs:

- **Paragraph Structure**
- **Writing a Topic Sentence**
- **Improving a Topic Sentence**
- **Supporting Details**
- **Developing Supporting Details**
- **Organizing Paragraphs**
- **Writing a Concluding Sentence**

PARAGRAPH STRUCTURE

A **paragraph** is a series of related sentences that make a single point about one subject. That single point is called the **main idea**, and it is usually stated in the **topic sentence** of a paragraph. The topic sentence often begins a paragraph, though it may also be at the end or in the middle of a paragraph. The **supporting details** in the paragraph explain the main idea. If the topic sentence does not end the paragraph, a **concluding sentence** can bring the paragraph to a close, and if appropriate, lead into the next paragraph.

An easy way to understand the structure of a paragraph is to compare it to a table. The main idea is like the table top. Just as the table's purpose is to provide a flat surface for writing or eating, the paragraph's purpose is to tell the reader about the main idea. Of course, without legs, the table top will not stand. In a similar way, the main idea must be supported by details, examples, and explanations. Finally, a table that rocks on an uneven floor makes people wonder if objects they place on it will fall off. Similarly, a paragraph that does not provide a clear conclusion may leave the reader unsure if the supporting details relate to each other.

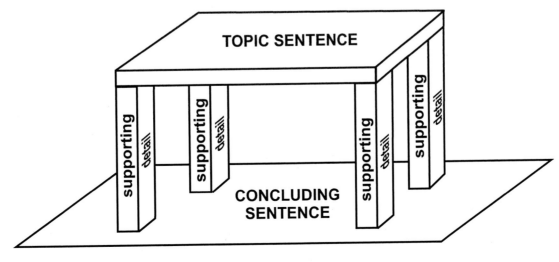

Writing a well-organized paragraph may seem difficult, but do you realize that you talk in paragraphs every day? Here is an example of a paragraph spoken by a cheerleading coach at the season's first practice.

Gather around here and listen up! **If you really want to be cheerleaders, you have to be ready to stretch yourself to the limit!** *Be sure you really want to do this, girls! You will need to be at practice every day after school. There will be no time for any other extracurricular activities! All of you must be ready to give of yourselves and endure pain as you never have before! You will also need to rely on each other. Some of you will be learning how to trust someone else for the first time in your lives. Above all, this job will bring out your character and show you what you're made of. Now, if you still feel up to the task, I want to see you here tomorrow evening at five o'clock, ready to work hard.*

Though spoken, the coach's instruction is like a well-written paragraph. It states the main idea in a topic sentence (indicated in bold) and then supports that idea by describing how the cheerleaders will need to "stretch themselves." The coach concludes by challenging the cheerleaders to action. The speech has overall **coherence** in that all the ideas and sentences relate to one another.

STRUCTURE OF A PARAGRAPH

Topic Sentence (Introduction)

↓

Supporting Details (examples, reasons, testimony, observations)

↓

Concluding Sentence (Summary)

PRACTICE 1: PARAGRAPH STRUCTURE

All of the sentences in each series make a paragraph, but they may not be in order. For each sentence, write T if the sentence is the topic sentence, S if the sentence supports the topic sentence, and C if the sentence concludes or summarizes the paragraph.

1. A. Constantly surrounded by beeping faxes, ringing cell phones, and flashing computer screens, many business people are sitting down at the end of the day to enjoy some quiet time with knitting needles and a big ball of yarn.
    B. Men and women with fast-paced, high-powered careers are turning to knitting as a way to unwind.
    C. So, as you speed through modern society, remember, knitting isn't just for Grandma anymore!
    D. Besides the peace and quiet, these knitting professionals say they find it refreshing to focus on the process of creating something, instead of looking only at deadlines and finished products.

    Sentence A _____   Sentence C _____
    Sentence B _____   Sentence D _____

Copyright © American Book Company

2. A. As she climbed the stairs, her nose was filled with the musty smell of old things.
   B. She walked to the door of her old refuge: the attic.
   C. Times at home had always been happy, but now Sheila needed a break.
   D. The memories of good times made the present situation seem bearable.
   E. Sheila dusted off an old picture frame and found a picture of her mother, smiling.

   Sentence A _____   Sentence C _____   Sentence E _____
   Sentence B _____   Sentence D _____

3. A. With the sale of new each bike, he offered a monthly maintenance program.
   B. These regular check-ups kept the bikes in good working condition and brought customers back to the store where they could see new products he was selling.
   C. The success of Alek's young business shows the importance of keeping the customer happy.
   D. His work in other bicycle shops had shown him that a successful business is based on quality products and good service.
   E. With several years experience under his belt, Alek Siegers established a new bicycle shop in Aspen, Colorado.

   Sentence A _____   Sentence C _____   Sentence E _____
   Sentence B _____   Sentence D _____

4. A. While Brad, Katya, and Willy were strolling down Eighth Street, they heard a disturbing noise.
   B. They looked up and saw an elderly woman calling out from a second floor window, "Help me, please."
   C. The look on the woman's face propelled the three teens up the stairs to her door.
   D. Within minutes, police officers arrived and commended the teens for their quick thinking.
   E. Immediately, Katya called 911, while Brad checked the man's pulse, and Willy tried to reassure the woman.
   F. The woman could not speak but brought them to the kitchen where her husband lay on the floor.

   Sentence A _____   Sentence C _____   Sentence E _____
   Sentence B _____   Sentence D _____   Sentence F _____

5. A. Training involves many hours of lifting weights and running sprints.
   B. Without this preparation, performance drops and injuries are more of a risk.
   C. Like the other athletes you see at the Olympics, javelin throwers deserve respect.
   D. The javelin is not a very heavy object, but throwing it long distances requires great arm and leg strength.
   E. Javelin throwing may look easy on T.V., but in reality, it is a very demanding sport.

   Sentence A _____   Sentence C _____   Sentence E _____
   Sentence B _____   Sentence D _____

Copyright © American Book Company

WRITING A TOPIC SENTENCE

The previous section shows that a paragraph is organized around a single idea, called the **main idea**. The statement of the main idea is called the **topic sentence**. The topic sentence tells the reader two important pieces of information:

    1) **the subject of the paragraph**
    2) **what the author wants the reader to know about that subject**

As a writer, you can use these statements to help you develop a topic sentence. Begin by answering the following two questions:

What is the subject of the paragraph?
What do I want the reader to know about that subject?

Then, use the answers to these questions to form a topic sentence. For example,

Subject:	fuel-efficient cars
Want reader to know:	help the environment
Sentence:	Buying a fuel-efficient car is one way you can help the environment.

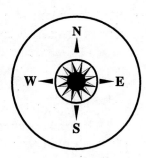

This simple method of forming a topic sentence can help you stay focused in your writing. The topic sentence is like your compass while you write. It tells you what direction you want to go. Then, if you feel yourself getting lost in your writing, you can return to your topic sentence to get your bearings. For each sentence in a paragraph, ask the two questions above. If the sentence doesn't relate in some way to the subject and what you want the reader to know about the subject, it doesn't belong in the paragraph.

> *The topic sentence states the subject of the paragraph and what the author wants the reader to know about that subject.*

PRACTICE 2: WRITING A TOPIC SENTENCE

For each of the following, write a topic sentence based on the subject and what you want the reader to know.

1.   Subject: baseball cards
       Want reader to know: it's an interesting hobby

Topic Sentence: _____

_____

Copyright © American Book Company

2.. Subject: televisions in classrooms
Want reader to know: provide learning opportunities

Topic Sentence: _____

_____

3. Subject: refugees in the United States
Want reader to know: struggle without knowledge of English

Topic Sentence: _____

_____

4. Subject: exercise
Want reader to know: important for good health

Topic Sentence: _____

_____

5. Subject: school uniforms
Want reader to know: decrease learning distractions

Topic Sentence: _____

_____

IMPROVING A TOPIC SENTENCE

The previous exercise may make writing a topic sentence seem easy, but writing a *good* topic sentence is a little more challenging. It is like deciding the best way to begin a conversation. Some people are very good at starting a conversation and keeping it going. They have a talent for inviting others into dialogue by picking a good topic and introducing it in an interesting way. When you write, you are starting a conversation with the reader. The topic sentence provides the basis for this conversation. A good topic sentence should present a **single idea** that is **broad enough** to **invite discussion**.

1. **Single Idea.** Because a paragraph is focused on one idea, the topic sentence also should be limited to a single idea. The sentence should have only one subject and one verb.

A. **Incorrect:** *Baseball players and lawyers get paid too much for the work they do.*

This sentence has two subjects: baseball players and lawyers. The support needed for this sentence requires more than one paragraph. Choose one subject for one paragraph.

Correct: *Baseball players get paid too much for the work they do.*
Correct: *Lawyers get paid too much for the work they do.*

B. **Incorrect:** *The Internet provides computer users with a vast source of information and creates worldwide marketing opportunities for businesses.*

The Internet is a single subject, but the sentence describes two services provided by the Internet. Either service provides the basis for a good paragraph.

> **Correct:** *The Internet provides computer users with a vast source of information.*
> **Correct:** *The Internet creates worldwide marketing opportunities for businesses.*

C. **Incorrect:** *Young children bring parents great joy as well as tremendous responsibility.*

This sentence introduces two ideas. One idea is that young children bring parents great joy. The other is that young children are a big responsibility for parents. Both ideas should not be in the same topic sentence.

> **Correct:** *Young children bring great joy to parents.*
> **Correct:** *Young children bring parents tremendous responsibility.*

2. **Broad Enough.** The topic sentence must be broad enough so that it can be supported by details. A topic sentence that is, itself, a detail has no place to go.

A. **Detail:** *Baking soda absorbs household odors in carpets and kitchens.*
    Detail: *Lemon juice lightens stains and cuts grease.*
    Topic: *Natural household products can be used for effective cleaning.*

The third sentence is broad enough to be supported by the details of the first two sentences. However, the first two sentences are too specific to be discussed in a paragraph. The same is true of the next example.

B. **Detail:** *Genetic engineers have succeeded in cloning farm animals.*
    Detail: *Lawyers use DNA tests in criminal court cases.*
    Topic: *In recent years, genetic research has produced astounding, yet practical, results.*

3. **Invites Discussion.** A good topic sentence makes the reader want to continue reading. It usually begins the paragraph and should invite the reader to consider the writer's topic.

A. **Weak:** *I went to Florida last year.*
    Good: *Florida is the ideal place to go for a winter vacation.*

Copyright © American Book Company

The weak topic sentence doesn't have any energy or movement. There's no clear direction to go in writing, and the reader may not want to follow you anyway. A good topic sentence makes the reader ask questions and want to read more, as in the following two examples.

B. Weak: *My uncle drives a black Nissan 300 ZX.*
    Good: *People often choose a particular car as a reflection of their personality.*

C. Weak: *Autumn leaves are often multicolored.*
    Good: *I love how the leaves on the trees explode into color each fall.*

> **A good topic sentence must be a single idea that is broad enough to invite discussion.**

PRACTICE 3: CHOOSING A TOPIC SENTENCE

For each group of sentences, decide which is a good topic sentence. Then, describe why the others are not as effective.

1. a. I had never seen so much trash in all my life! _____

    b. The trash began piling up. _____

    c. Last summer, I worked for a trash collection company. _____

2. a. It's time to plant the garden and start watching baseball again. _____

    b. Irises and azaleas are beginning to bloom in the garden. _____

    c. The fresh smell of a newly planted garden is the best part of spring. _____

3. a. Bobby Knight is a demanding and controversial coach._____

    b. Bobby Knight is a unique personality in college basketball. _____

    c. Bobby Knight lost the respect of many when, in the
        middle of a game, he threw a chair across the basketball court. _____

4. a. This has been a dry summer. _____

    b. Rainfall in the metro region is two inches below normal. _____

    c. This summer's drought may put water supplies in danger. _____

5. a. Modern rap is rooted in traditional African music. _____

    b. Modern rap has led to creative innovations in music. _____

    c. My brother listens to rap music all the time. _____

SUPPORTING DETAILS

An effective topic sentence starts your conversation with the reader, but it is up to you to continue the conversation by providing a clear, logical explanation of the main idea. **Supporting details** are specific statements that are related to the topic of the paragraph, but they do more than just restate the main idea.

1. **Supporting details are more than restatements of the topic sentence.** They provide reasons and examples that show why the main idea is true. Look at the following two examples.

Example 1: *Researchers have proven that smoking is bad for your health. Many researchers have determined smoking is unhealthy. In addition, researchers have publicized smoking's harmful components.*

In Example 1, the underlined topic sentence is *not* supported with details. Instead, the next two sentences simply restate the topic sentence in different words.

Example 2: *Researchers have proven that smoking is bad for your health. The American Medical Association has issued several warnings about the increased risk of lung cancer associated with smoking. In addition, the* New England Journal of Medicine *has issued its own separate findings verifying this same association.*

In Example 2, the same underlined topic sentence is supported by details. The writer cites both the American Medical Association and the *New England Journal of Medicine* as examples of research which has shown the relationship between lung cancer and smoking.

2. **Supporting details are related to the topic.** If the details digress from the topic, these unrelated ideas can weaken the coherence of the paragraph and confuse the reader.

Example 3: *It is easy to learn a new language. Sometimes it's hard to find someone who speaks another language. It's also fun to learn martial arts. Sometimes I just can't learn how to memorize things.*

Each of the sentences in Example 3 may have one or two words in common, but they all refer to different topics. Each sentence should relate to the idea "It is easy to learn a new language."

Example 4: *It is easy to learn a new language. Right now, you can learn a language by taking an elective course in high school. Then, if you go to college you may have the opportunity to live in a foreign country as an exchange student. All along, you can join chat rooms on the Internet or conversation meetings in your area that will help you practice speaking your new language.*

In Example 4, the supporting sentences in the paragraph explain and relate to the underlined topic sentence. The sentences provide specific examples of ways you can learn a foreign language.

Copyright © American Book Company

3. Supporting details are specific, not general, statements. The topic sentence is a general statement, but you should explain it in detail. Be as specific as you can.

Example 5: *Opinion polls question small samples of the population in order to indicate larger trends. An important part of polling is making sure that different kinds of people are represented. Even though this country is made up of many different kinds of people, opinion polls are pretty accurate.*

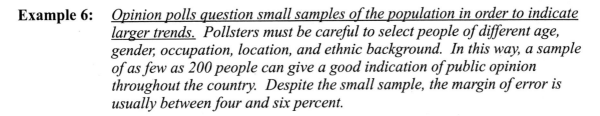

All of the sentences in Example 5 discuss opinion polls, but each one is general enough to be a topic for its own paragraph. They are related to the same idea, but they don't focus on one aspect of that idea.

Example 6: *Opinion polls question small samples of the population in order to indicate larger trends. Pollsters must be careful to select people of different age, gender, occupation, location, and ethnic background. In this way, a sample of as few as 200 people can give a good indication of public opinion throughout the country. Despite the small sample, the margin of error is usually between four and six percent.*

The author of Example 6 chose one general statement as the topic sentence (underlined) and supported it with specific details that emphasize the accuracy of polls based only on small samples of the population. Each supporting sentence elaborates on this one idea.

> ***Supporting details are specific statements that are related to the topic of the paragraph, but they do more than just restate the main idea.***

PRACTICE 4: SUPPORTING DETAILS

Read each group of sentences below. If the group forms a well-developed paragraph, write "Correct." If the group restates the topic sentence, contains unrelated ideas, or uses general statements instead of specifics, state the problem, and rewrite the paragraph on a separate sheet of paper.

1. Swimming is really the healthiest exercise anyone can do. Jumping rope is also healthy, and it's a lot of fun. Sometimes just talking on the phone with friends can be fun, but you don't get much exercise. Going to the movies can be amusing, and if you walk there, it might be healthy. Just don't get butter on your popcorn because that's not healthy.

2. Something should be done about the cafeteria food because it tastes bad. Every time I gobble a mouthful, the taste is foul. Everyone agrees that the food tastes bad, and they bring in sack lunches instead. The food just does not taste good.

3. Scientists have a new theory to explain the mass extinction of aquatic life 186 million years ago. Using chemical analysis, researchers have determined that a large amount of methane gas was released from ocean floor sediment about that time. The methane combined with oxygen in the ocean and formed carbon dioxide. Without oxygen available, marine life could not breathe. Researchers believe this was the cause of death for many ancient underwater creatures.

Copyright © American Book Company

4.   I enjoy the smell of the air after a good rain. The air smells very good when the rain ends. After the water comes down from the clouds, the air smells very clean. Everyone enjoys the smell outside after a long soaking downpour. Nothing refreshes the air like a spring rain.

 5.   Many people wonder whether there is life on other planets in the universe. All around the world, people claim to see U.F.O.'s. The idea of creatures from other planets visiting Earth has been the topic of many books and movies. Science fiction clubs are very popular and often have large annual meetings.

DEVELOPING SUPPORTING DETAILS

A good way to develop a list of details to support your main idea is to consider what questions a reader might ask about your topic sentence. Here is an example:

Topic Sentence: Florida is the ideal place to go for a winter vacation.

Reader May Ask: Where in Florida?
How do you know it's ideal?
What makes it ideal?
What kinds of things can you do there?
What if I like to go snow skiing?

By answering these questions, you can develop a list of supporting ideas for your topic.

Possible Answers: Panama City
went last year for annual vacation
good seafood, great night life, beautiful beaches
swimming, snorkeling
water skiing

From this list, you can develop a paragraph like the following:

Panama City, Florida

Florida is the ideal place to go for a winter vacation. Last year, our family spent its annual vacation on the white beaches of Panama City. During the day, we snorkeled, swam, and water skied in the clear, warm waters of the Gulf of Mexico. In the evenings, we enjoyed fresh seafood at the small, local restaurants. At night, we joined other vacationers from around the world in various festivities sponsored by our hotel. Every year we travel to a new vacation spot, but the beauty and excitement of Florida will bring us back next year.

Supporting details provide answers to questions the reader may have about a topic sentence.

      Copyright © American Book Company

PRACTICE 5: DEVELOPING SUPPORTING DETAILS

For each of the following topic sentences, develop a list of at least three supporting details. The first topic is completed as an example.

1. The fresh smell of a newly planted garden is the best part of spring.

   a. *The smell of new growth contrasts the long months of dead winter.*

   b. *Early budding flowers have a gentle fragrance.*

   c. *Freshly tilled earth has a unique smell.*

2. Parents have a tremendous responsibility in raising young children.

   a. _____

   b. _____

   c. _____

3. Televisions in classrooms provide a wide range of learning opportunities.

   a. _____

   b. _____

   c. _____

4. Refugees who come to the United States face many difficulties if they don't speak English.

   a. _____

   b. _____

   c. _____

5. Baseball players get paid too much for the work they do.

   a. _____

   b. _____

   c. _____

Copyright © American Book Company

ORGANIZING PARAGRAPHS

Now that you have a topic sentence and a list of supporting details, you must decide how you want to organize your paragraph. Just like the table we discussed at the beginning of this chapter, a paragraph is not put together haphazardly. It has structure and organization to make it stand. And just like there are different types of tables, there are different ways to organize paragraphs, such as **time order**, **spatial order**, **order of importance** and **contrasting ideas**.

Time Order

Time order is especially important when you are writing a narrative. A story doesn't make sense when the events are not presented in the proper sequence. Here is an example:

> *I arrived after the speaker had begun her presentation. As I was running down the hill, I remembered that I had left my car keys on the kitchen table. When I started the car, I saw the clock, and I knew I was going to be late. I had to go back and get my keys.*

The lack of organization in this paragraph makes it very difficult to follow the story line. See below how organizing the passage in a time sequence makes it much easier to read and understand.

> *As I was running down the hill, I remembered that I had left my car keys on the kitchen table. I had to go back and get my keys. When I started the car, I saw the clock, and I knew I was going to be late. I arrived after the speaker had begun her presentation.*

You can also use time order to organize other types of writing, including persuasive writing. Review the paragraph in the last section about vacationing in Florida. Notice how the details are organized according to time order.

Spatial Order

When you describe a scene or a location, you can sometimes use **spatial order** to arrange your ideas in a paragraph. Imagine yourself holding a camcorder and moving it in every direction. You can order your observations from **top to bottom**, **left to right**, **clockwise**, **near to far**, **front to back**, **inside to outside**, **east to west**, **north to south**, etc., and all of these directions *reversed* (e.g., **bottom to top**). Read the following description of a horse organized in spatial order.

> *When I saw the horse, I knew I was looking at a creature of great athletic beauty and ability. The horse's head was finely shaped, as if sculpted by an artist. On either side of its head, the eyes were alert and far-seeing. The ears were pointed and moved attentively to the slightest sound. The horse's neck was crested in a proud arch, and its muscular shoulders tapered down to powerful legs. The spine of the horse was perfectly aligned, and the back legs were unblemished and moved freely. The hindquarters of the horse were well rounded, and the horse's tail flowed like silk in the wind. In short, this horse was a magnificent animal.*

Copyright © American Book Company

Look at the picture of the horse on the previous page. Does it make sense from the description you just read? If not, what additional details or observations would improve the description?

In the passage, the details of the horse are organized in a front to back order. First, the writer discusses the horse's head, along with the eyes and ears. Second, the writer provides details about the neck, shoulders, and front legs. Third, the writer describes the spine and the back legs. Finally, the author tells us about the horse's hindquarters and tail.

Spatial order can also be an effective way to organize other kinds of writing, as you can see in the following example of persuasive writing.

It's time for the city to clean up Jones Park. As visitors enter the park, they are greeted by a broken sign that is smeared with graffiti. Next, they pass the pond where they must hold their noses because of the smell of decaying trash. If visitors make it past all of this, they reach the playground in the middle of the park. Here they find swings with ripped seats hanging limp beside slides with broken steps. The park in its current state is a hazardous waste area that must be cleaned up.

Order of Importance

The most common way to organize a paragraph is by **order of importance**. All of the details you include in your paragraph should be relevant to the topic and important to the reader. Some details, however, you will want to emphasize more than others. You can emphasize a certain idea by placing it either at the beginning or at the end of a paragraph. The following letter provides a good example.

Dear Aunt Jenny,

I would really like to spend the summer with you because I have never spent much time in Oregon. Also I am interested in earning some extra money for my college savings, and many jobs are available in your area. Most importantly, I really enjoy our short visits when we get together over the holidays, and I want to spend more time with you so we can be closer.

Please write back soon, and let me know what you think.

Love,
Sandra

In this letter, Sandra begins with a simple wish that may be of some interest to her aunt. Aunt Jenny would be more likely to respect Sandra's second reason. However, Sandra's desire for a closer relationship will make the greatest impression upon her aunt's decision.

Copyright © American Book Company

Of course, the letter could be arranged so that the most important idea comes first:

Dear Aunt Jenny,

    I would like to spend the summer with you because I really enjoy our short visits when we get together over the holidays, and I want to spend more time with you so we can be closer. I am also interested in earning some extra money for my college savings, and many jobs are available in your area. Besides, I have never spent much time in Oregon.
    Please write back soon, and let me know what you think.

Love,
Sandra

Sometimes you will want to start off with the most important idea. Other times you will want to "save the best for last." The decision is yours based upon your audience, topic, and personal preference.

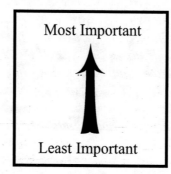

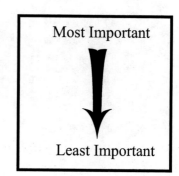

Contrasting Ideas

The Georgia High School Writing Test requires you to choose one side of an issue and convince the reader of the validity of your position. One good way to do this is to **contrast** your position with its opposite. In this kind of contrasting, you will point out differences and show why your position is better. For example, look at the paragraph below in which the writer is trying to convince his or her family about the best kind of pet to get.

    Since our family spends a lot of time traveling, a cat is definitely a better choice than a dog for a family pet. Dogs need to be let outside several times a day, while a cat knows how to use a litter box. Dogs also need to be fed regularly, whereas a cat can snack on one bowl of food for a few days. Dogs are very social animals and get lonely if they don't have people or other dogs to play with. Cats, on the other hand, are affectionate sometimes, but they can also get along just fine by themselves. A dog would not be treated well enough in our busy household. A cat would be much happier.

In this example, the writer contrasts the qualities of a dog with those of a cat. The writer points out the reasons why a cat would fit better in the family that likes to travel. Someone with a different family situation could write a paragraph like the following:

Copyright © American Book Company

For our young family, a dog would be a much better choice than a cat for a family pet. Dogs are social animals who love to be around people, especially kids. Cats, on the other hand, avoid crowds and often run from children. Dogs require regular feeding, which is a great opportunity to teach children responsibility. Cats require much less regular care. A dog offers great security for a home and family by barking when strangers approach. A cat can do little more than hiss at someone it doesn't like. A cat just doesn't offer our family the benefits provided by a dog.

This second paragraph shows how awareness of audience is important in writing. Different families have different needs and interests. Therefore, a cat may be the better choice for the first family, and a dog would be better for the second family.

> ***Paragraphs can be organized according to space, time, importance, or contrasting ideas.***

PRACTICE 6: ORGANIZING PARAGRAPHS

Look at the pictures below. Create a paragraph about these pictures, and write it on a separate sheet of paper. Make sure the sentences follow the order listed above the picture.

Time Order

Order of Importance

Spatial Order

Contrasting Ideas

PRACTICE 7: ORGANIZING PARAGRAPHS

Return to the list of supporting details you developed in Practice 5 on page 25. Put each list in order according to time, space, importance, or contrasting ideas.

WRITING A CONCLUDING SENTENCE

As you learned in the last section, the beginning and end of a paragraph are very important. Sometimes a topic sentence will end a paragraph, but often it comes at the beginning, in order to alert the reader to the main idea. In this case, the paragraph will end with a **concluding sentence**. The concluding sentence brings closure to the paragraph by providing a summary of the topic and the supporting details. It may also suggest what action the reader should take. If another paragraph follows, the concluding sentence serves as a link between the two paragraphs.

As we compare a paragraph to a table, we see that the concluding sentence is like the floor which provides a stable base on which the table can stand. A paragraph that lacks a concluding sentence may leave the reader uncertain and without a sense of closure. Read the example below to understand the importance of concluding sentences.

Example: *In the United Kingdom, there are cameras all over the place in large cities such as London, and it seems to help police fight crime. If a crime occurs, they can look at video footage to see what the criminal looks like. They can then show the footage on TV and citizens can report to the police if they recognize the person. With so many people traveling around the country on public transportation, the cameras can also help track down criminals there. There is also lots of crime in large cities in the United States, and it is often difficult to catch the criminals.*

This paragraph lacks an ending. The paragraph begins with an opinion about the effectiveness of cameras in the United Kingdom, followed by supporting sentences that back up this point. However, the lack of a conclusion leaves the reader wondering whether the paragraph is finished.

The addition of a concluding sentence like the following would make a big difference.

Concluding Sentence: *Since cameras have proven to be effective in the United Kingdom, I think we should convince our own communities that installing more cameras in public places will reduce crime and help us catch more criminals, making everyone feel safer as a result.*

This one sentence ties the paragraph together by summarizing the controlling idea and supporting details and urging the reader to take action. The reader may agree or disagree with the writer's ideas, but the reader has no doubt that the writer has brought the paragraph to a close.

> *A concluding sentence may achieve one or more of the following:*
>
> *Emphasize an important point;*
> *Provide a summary of the topic and details;*
> *Suggest a response for the reader;*
> *Link one paragraph to another.*

Copyright © American Book Company

PRACTICE 8: CONCLUDING SENTENCES

Read the following paragraphs. In the blanks after each paragraph, write a concluding sentence that best completes the topic discussed. If the paragraph contains a concluding sentence, write "Correct."

1.   The global economy is moving toward the East. By 2020, China is projected to have an economy that is roughly 1.5 times as large as the economy of the United States! In addition, Japan, India, and Indonesia will have production levels that rival the United States. Only four nations in Europe will even make the top twenty list of the world's largest economies.

_____

2.   The dancing craze is back in full force in the United States. After years of obscurity, swing music has made a rapid comeback. Also, the Latin rhythms of salsa, merengue, and cumbia can be heard in many cities. Two-stepping in clubs playing country music is also popular with the younger generation. In addition, the clubs playing techno, hip hop, and R&B music continue to draw larger crowds.

_____

3.   At the church pot luck dinner, each family competes to bring in the best entree and dessert. Mrs. Collin's chicken cacciatore was a fierce challenge to Mr. Ewing's homemade barbeque. Miss Laramie brought in two scrumptious apple pies that were gone in seconds, and everyone marveled at Miss Jenkin's homemade ice cream. This pot luck dinner was deliciously serious business.

_____

4.   Lifting weights is both mentally and physically demanding. It takes a great amount of concentration to lift large weights safely. Every lifter knows that form is crucial. The lifter must understand and visualize what he or she is doing during every second of a lift. People who do not exercise their mind in this manner end up with strains, sprains, and back and neck injuries.

_____

5.   The National Public Radio station in your city is a great educational resource. Because it receives funding from listeners, not big businesses, the station can offer diverse programming. You can hear informative and entertaining presentations about science, history, cultural movements, business trends, and film. In addition, the news programs provide longer, in-depth reports about major issues. Best of all, you can listen to all these great programs without those annoying commercials. Tune in to public radio today, and feed your mind with some high quality programs.

_____

PRACTICE 9: WRITING PARAGRAPHS

Use the topic sentences and supporting details from Practices 5 and 7 to write four well-organized paragraphs. Be sure each paragraph has a concluding sentence.

Copyright © American Book Company

CHAPTER 1 SUMMARY: WRITING PARAGRAPHS

STRUCTURE OF A PARAGRAPH

Topic Sentence (Introduction)

↓

Supporting Details (examples, reasons, testimony, observations)

↓

Concluding Sentence (Summary)

- *The topic sentence states the subject of the paragraph and what the author wants the reader to know about that subject.*

- *A good topic sentence must be a single idea that is broad enough to invite discussion.*

- *Supporting details are specific statements that are related to the topic of the paragraph, but they do more than just restate the main idea.*

- *Supporting details answer questions the reader may have.*

- *Paragraphs can be organized according to time, space, importance, or contrasting ideas.*

- *A concluding sentence may achieve one or more of the following:*

    Emphasize an important point;
    Provide a summary of the topic and details;
    Suggest a response for the reader;
    Link one paragraph to another.

Copyright © American Book Company

CHAPTER 1 REVIEW: WRITING PARAGRAPHS

Rewrite each unorganized group of sentences (1-5) in the form of a well-organized paragraph. Each group contains an unrelated idea that you must eliminate. Also, each group is missing a *topic sentence*, so you will need to create one and include it in your rewritten paragraph.

1.
   A. Neither the Republicans nor the Democrats are eager to tackle this issue.
   B. When considering the environment, most people think only about their own little world.
   C. They have to start going beyond the "What's in it for me?" attitude.
   D. The decisions we make have a big impact on the rest of the world.
   E. Citizens of this country need to realize that we are all part of a global community.

2.
   A. The owner of the resort had breakfast ready downstairs.
   B. To our right, three deer were drinking out of a small stream.
   C. Straight ahead, the colorful valley opened up for us.
   D. To our left, the sun pierced through the tall trees.
   E. We were deeply impressed with everything we saw from our cabin.

3.
   A. Our friends took the day off with us so we could go to the mall.
   B. The editors also warned us that we would need to find some place else to work if we ever did that again.
   C. Unfortunately for us, we did not know that ACME motors advertized in our newspaper.
   D. The editors pulled every copy from the newsstands before the public saw them.
   E. The story concerned the bad performance of ACME transmissions.

4.
   A. Something needs to be done, and soon.
   B. The problem is that costs keep skyrocketing while service is plummeting.
   C. Doctors used to make house calls.
   D. Meanwhile, patients spend more and more time waiting, and less and less time talking with the doctor.
   E. Doctors order more and more high-tech tests that increase medical bills.

5.
   A. In addition, you are the first person to be unhappy with our product.
   B. We found, however, that it was in perfect working condition.
   C. The letter you sent said that the product was broken.
   D. Have you ever considered selling those gadgets yourself?
   E. Based on these reasons, I am sure you can understand why there is no possibility of a refund.

Rewrite each group of sentences (6-10) in the form of a well-organized paragraph. For each group, you will need to eliminate one unrelated idea and create a concluding sentence.

6. A. Donna aimed the shot high and swished the basketball through the hoop.
   B. She passed the ball to Donna the first chance she had.
   C. Donna and Jenna want to go to the same college.
   D. Jenna certainly gave Donna an assist on the first play of the game.
   E. Next, Jenna shielded the other players from Donna as she took her shot.

7. A. Calligraphy is one of the most difficult forms of art I know.
   B. Each stroke of the pen has to be perfect.
   C. For example, the ink runs if the stroke is too slow.
   D. Also, the letters have gaps if the stroke is too fast.
   E. Because of the precision required, it can take many months to master a single alphabet in calligraphy.
   F. I hope to open a business selling calligraphy pens and ink supplies.

8. A. Some parents don't have time to coach sports for children.
   B. They said the boy wasn't getting enough playing time.
   C. This may be extreme, but how often do some parents start screaming at officials who make a bad call?
   D. Recently, the father and uncle of a football player in California beat up the boy's coach.
   E. Sometimes parents get carried away by the competition of children's sports.

9. A. The dome's shape is especially resistant to storms and earthquakes because the foundation supports all portions of the structure.
   B. A few nonconformists are building dome style homes because of their stability and energy efficiency.
   C. The lack of walls in a dome-shaped house allows more equal distribution of heating and cooling, making it more energy efficient.
   D. Other people enjoy traditional four-sided brick homes.

10. A. This move brings Nuke-Clean closer to one of its big customers–the nuclear plant down the river.
    B. It also brings it closer to my neighborhood.
    C. Some people in the neighborhood don't mind, but I think we should take action now.
    D. Nuke-Clean wants to move its operation to Smith County, so it can clean clothes that are contaminated with radiation.
    E. The nuclear plant in Chernobyl was shut down recently.

Copyright © American Book Company

The paragraphs below (11-15) may be missing a topic sentence or a concluding sentence. Also, they may contain supporting details that restate the topic or describe unrelated ideas. For each paragraph, identify the problem. Then, rewrite the paragraph to make it complete.

11.   Getting the right tennis shoe for school can be an important decision. Getting blue jeans to fit is difficult sometimes. Whenever I try to tie-dye my t-shirts, they always turn out brown! My skin feels better after a long dip in the swimming pool. In summary, comfortable tennis shoes are vital for school survival.

12.   Exercising will improve blood flow to the brain and condition the muscles and bones to support the body under stress. Also, a proper diet will ensure that the brain and other parts of the body are supplied with the proper nutrients. Third, a proper amount of sleep will keep the receptors in the brain connected for maximum efficiency. These three life activities in proper balance will keep the body and mind in shape for each day.

13.   Misha Patel enjoyed his visit to Disney World in July. The July visit to Disney World was very enjoyable for Misha. Disney World provided Misha with many interesting experiences. In short, Misha was very happy experiencing many of the attractions offered at Disney World.

14.   Global warming is a very real and measurable phenomenon. Over the past century, glaciers near the poles have receded. In addition, the polar ice caps have thinned up to 40% from their previous thickness. Finally, air temperatures have warmed over 1°Celsius.

15.   The world now produces more than enough food to feed every man, woman, and child currently living. However, land useful for farming is not evenly distributed. Another challenge lies in lack of transportation to areas where there is no arable land. Furthermore, many nations lacking the arable land also lack the resources necessary to purchase the food they need. Together, these factors point to a problem in food distribution, not a lack of food.

ADDITIONAL ACTIVITIES: WRITING PARAGRAPHS

Topic Sentences

1   Review photographs, advertisements, paintings, or cartoons in books or magazines or on the Internet. Make copies of four of these visual expressions. Then write topic sentences based on these examples. Seek feedback on your topic sentences from your teacher or from other students. Do the topic sentences focus on a single idea? Are they broad enough to be supported by details and examples? Do they invite discussion?

2.   Write four topic sentences based on topics of your choosing. You can also use any of the following topics to help you get started.

school buses	**losing weight**	**tattoos**	**drinking**
favorite food	**nose rings**	**pet peeve**	**cure a cold**
girlfriend	**gossip**	**ideal job**	**favorite entertainer**
boyfriend	**my dream**	**worst job**	

Exchange your topic sentences with your teacher or with other students. Do the topic sentences focus on a single idea? Are they broad enough to be supported by details and examples? Do they invite discussion?

Supporting Details and Organizing Paragraphs

3.   Choose four of your best topic sentences from number 1 or number 2 above. Write four to six sentences that support these topic sentences. Make sure your details relate to the topic, are specific, and avoid restating the topic sentence.

Use a different way to organize each paragraph. In other words, use time order for one paragraph, spatial order for your next paragraph, order of importance for another paragraph, and contrasting ideas for your last paragraph.

Concluding Sentences

4.   Write a concluding sentence for each of your four paragraphs. Make sure that your concluding sentence summarizes the topic sentence and supporting details in each paragraph.

Final Activity

5.   Turn in your completed paragraphs for feedback from your teacher or tutor. Revise them as needed. For further practice in writing paragraphs, repeat steps 1-5, using different topics.

Note: **For more instruction and practice for various aspects of writing, visit the Web sites listed in Appendix B (pages 185-188).**

Copyright © American Book Company

Chapter 2
Writing to Persuade

The Georgia High School Writing Test requires you to write a **persuasive essay** in which you must try to convince the reader to agree with your point of view. In order to do this effectively, you must be aware of the following aspects of writing which you will study and practice in this chapter:

- **Author's Purpose**
- **Audience**
- **Language and Tone**

- **Using Persuasive Language**
- **Building an Argument**

AUTHOR'S PURPOSE

There are many reasons why an author puts pen to paper or clicks away at the keyboard. Just think of the reasons why you write: you write essays for English class because the teacher requires it; you may write a note in a birthday card to your mother to express your love; or you may send e-mails to Internet friends just to keep in touch. Every author writes for a specific purpose. You can infer the **author's purpose** from the way an author writes. See if you can determine the author's purpose in the following two paragraphs.

Example 1:   *The common opossum is the only kind of opossum found in the United States. This species grows about as big as a house cat. It has rough grayish-white hair, a long snout, dark eyes, and big hairless ears. This opossum has a long tail that does not have much hair on it. The animal can hang upside down by wrapping its tail around a tree branch. Its teeth and claws are sharp.*

Example 2:   *One warm fall evening, our son Tom went out to the garage to feed the cat. Suddenly we heard him yell out, "A rat! A Texas-sized rat!" His older brother Joey went to investigate and reported back, "Sure enough, Mom. It is a rat!" Finally, Barb and I went to look at this "rat." When the little critter turned around to see us gawking, we realized that it was a 'possum . . . a fat 'possum.*

Both paragraphs discuss opossums, but they do so in very different ways. **Example 1** provides basic information about the physical features of one type of opossum. Though the paragraph contains descriptive words, there is no dialogue and no action. This paragraph would fit well in a science textbook. The author's purpose is **to inform**.

Example 2, on the other hand, describes characters and events with expressive words and interesting dialogue. It is part of a brief story about a surprising and funny event. Perhaps you would find it in a book of short stories. The author's purpose is **to entertain**.

Copyright © American Book Company

The ability to determine the author's purpose for writing enhances your reading comprehension. In addition, being clear about your purpose as an author will make your writing more effective. Become familiar with the following list of purposes for writing so that you may better understand the reasons why authors write.

Purpose	Definition	Reading Selection
To inform	To present facts and details	"Ocean Fishes"
To entertain	To amuse or offer enjoyment	"Time I Slipped in the Mud"
To persuade	To urge action on an issue	"Raise Penalties for Polluters"
To instruct	To teach concepts and facts	"Tips for Healthy Living"
To create suspense	To convey uncertainty	"Will Tom Win the Race?"
To motivate	To inspire to act	"You Can Lose Weight!"
To cause doubt	To be skeptical	"Are Adults Responsible?"
To describe an event	To narrate	"My Trip to Mobile"
To teach a lesson	To furnish knowledge	"Mastering Exponents"
To introduce a character	To describe a person's traits	"First Look at Captain Nemo"
To create a mood	To establish atmosphere	"Gloom in the House of Usher"
To relate an adventure	To tell an exciting story	"Lost in a Cave"
To share a personal experience	To tell about an event in your life	"The Time I Learned to Share"
To describe feelings	To communicate emotions through words	"When My Dog Died"

The Georgia High School Writing Test asks you to write a **persuasive essay**. In other words, your purpose for writing is to convince or influence the reader to agree with your point of view. Your goal is not only to inform the reader but also to show the reader that your viewpoint is correct. We will discuss the specifics of persuasion later in this chapter.

> *Your purpose for the Georgia High School Writing Test is to persuade.*

PRACTICE 1: AUTHOR'S PURPOSE

Based on the list of author's purposes, identify the author's purpose for the following reading passages. Then discuss your choices with your class or with your instructor.

1.   The fire crackled musically. From it swelled light smoke. Overhead the foliage moved softly. The leaves, with their faces turned toward the blaze, were colored shifting hues of silver, often edged with red. Far off to the right, through a window in the forest, could be seen a handful of stars lying, like glittering pebbles, on the black level of the night.

                                        – Stephen Crane, *Red Badge of Courage*

A.	To describe an event	C.	To persuade
B.	To create a mood	D.	To teach a lesson

Copyright © American Book Company

2.   Columbus' own successful voyage in 1492 prompted a papal bull dividing the globe between rivals Spain and Portugal. But the Portuguese protested that the pope's line left them too little Atlantic sea room for their voyages to India. The line was shifted 270 leagues westward in 1494 by the Treaty of Tordesillas. Thus, wittingly or not, the Portuguese gained Brazil and gave their language to more than half the people of South America.

A.   To teach a lesson
B.   To describe feelings
C.   To relate an adventure
D.   To inform

3.   Twelve-year-old Nadia told us a seemingly unbelievable story about her family's journey to the United States. In Romania, her father was involved in the politics of Romania, opposing the communist regime of Ceausescu. Because of death threats made against her family, Nadia and her family had to leave the country in the middle of the night. They had arranged for a boat to meet them so they could sail the Black Sea to freedom in Bulgaria. Because they left in a hurry, they took nothing with them except their clothes. The boat never came, so they swam into the sea until a boat from Bulgaria discovered her family swimming. All of them survived the swim except for Nadia's little brother, Dimitry. From that country, they obtained refugee status and traveled to the United States. Nadia is very grateful to be living here, and after hearing her story, so are we.

A.   To instruct
B.   To describe an event
C.   To relate an adventure
D.   To persuade

4.   Hand grippers can help give your arms those bulging biceps you're after, but only if they offer enough resistance. If you can squeeze them repeatedly for one to two minutes, and your hands don't get tired, they're too weak for you. You can keep buying stronger ones or make something at home that can do the same job.

A.   To instruct
B.   To persuade
C.   To describe an event
D.   To entertain

5.   My family came to America in 1985. No one spoke a word of English. In school, I was in an English as a Second Language class with other foreign-born children. My class was so overcrowded that it was impossible for the teacher to teach English properly. I dreaded going to school each morning because of the fear of not understanding what people were saying and the fear of being laughed at.

– Yu-Lan (Mary) Ying, an eyewitness account about learning English

A.   To cause doubt
B.   To entertain
C.   To share a personal experience
D.   To create suspense

Copyright © American Book Company

PRACTICE 2: AUTHOR'S PURPOSE

A.   In a group or on your own, review six articles from newspapers or magazines. Using the list of purposes for writing from this section, identify the author's purpose in each selection. Exchange your passages with a classmate to see if he/she identifies the same purpose. Then, discuss your findings with the class or with your teacher.

B.   Choose two or more purposes listed in the chart of purposes for writing. Write paragraphs that emphasize each purpose. Without revealing your purposes, share your paragraphs with your classmates or teacher. See if they can identify your intended purposes.

AUDIENCE

Once you are clear about your purpose for writing, you must consider your **audience**–the person(s) who will read what you write. Unless you are writing in your journal or taking notes in class, you are always writing for a particular audience. It may be your teacher, a friend, your parents, or a manager at work. Knowing your audience gives you important information including the **audience's interest**, the **audience's prior knowledge**, the **audience's vocabulary**, and **what the audience needs to know**. This information helps you write more effectively, especially when you are writing to persuade.

Read the following two paragraphs written by the same person. Try to develop a picture of the audience that the writer had in mind.

Example 1:   *Since you're in the market for a new car, I wanted to tell you about mine. My new car is the best one I've owned. It's a 2000 Mustang. It's got a 5.0 L overhead cam engine with multi-port fuel injection. It can do 0-60 mph in 5.5 seconds. With that much engine, passing cars on the highway is a breeze, but handling corners on back roads is a little trickier than with my old Honda CRX. I love the rush I get when I'm cruising around with my new wheels. You should consider buying one, too.*

Example 2:   *Since you're in the market for a new car, I wanted to tell you about mine. My new car is the best one I've owned. It's a 2000 Mustang. This sporty two-door is canary yellow with electric blue racing stripes and silver mag wheels. It has cordovan leather seats and a Bose sound system. The sunroof is the perfect finishing touch. You should see the looks I get when I'm cruising around with my new wheels. You should consider buying one, too.*

In both paragraphs, the author is telling someone about a new car, but each paragraph includes very different details about the car. Based on these differences, how would you describe the intended audience of each paragraph? What evidence is there for your description?

Audience Interest

How does the writer try to catch the audience's interest in each paragraph? Clearly, the first paragraph is intended for a reader who is interested in a car's power and performance. So, the writer describes the car's engine, as well as the car's speed and handling. The second paragraph, on the other hand, mentions nothing about performance. The writer assumes that the audience is concerned with appearance and style, so the description focuses on colors and high-priced options.

40   Copyright © American Book Company

Audience Knowledge

What does the writer assume that the audience already knows? Since the reader of the first paragraph is interested in performance, the writer assumes that the reader knows what a Ford Mustang is and that going 0-60 mph in 5.5 seconds is fast. The reader of the second paragraph may need the author to describe the Mustang as a "sporty two-door," but the reader understands well the stunning colors and fine accessories of the new car.

Audience Vocabulary

What kinds of words will the audience be familiar with and understand easily? The writer expects the reader of the first paragraph to know technical terms like "5.0 L" and "multi-port fuel injection." While these terms may speak loudly and clearly to the reader of the first paragraph, they may mean nothing to the reader of the second paragraph who appreciates "cordovan leather" and a "Bose sound system." Likewise, the reader of the first paragraph may have no use for these terms since they have nothing to do with power or performance.

What the Audience Should Know

What does the writer want the audience to know? In both paragraphs, the writer wants to share excitement about a new car purchase in order to encourage readers to purchase the same kind of car. The writer shares information that will be of interest to two kinds of audiences and that will encourage readers to purchase a Ford Mustang.

> *Your audience for the Georgia High School Writing Test may be parents, students, or local officials, but professional readers will grade your essay.*

Professional readers will grade your essay for the Georgia High School Writing Test. However, the writing prompt may ask you to address a particular audience, such as parents, teachers, other students, or the editor of a local newspaper. Considering your audience will help you write a more effective essay.

PRACTICE 3: AUDIENCE

For each of the following topics, describe the interest, knowledge, and vocabulary of the given audience, as well as what you think the audience should know.

1. Topic: Parental Advisory stickers on music CD's   Audience: parents

Audience Interest _interested in the welfare of their children_

Audience Knowledge _unfamiliar with specific artists, but aware of rude music_

Audience Vocabulary _some knowledge of teen vocabulary, but mostly not_

Audience Should Know _parents, not record companies, need to take responsibility_

Copyright © American Book Company

2.   Topic: Parental Advisory stickers on music CD's   Audience: students

Audience Interest _____

Audience Knowledge _____

Audience Vocabulary _____

Audience Should Know _____

3.   Topic: high salaries of professional athletes   Audience: baseball player

Audience Interest _____

Audience Knowledge _____

Audience Vocabulary _____

Audience Should Know _____

4.   Topic: high salaries of professional athletes   Audience: stadium worker

Audience Interest _____

Audience Knowledge _____

Audience Vocabulary _____

Audience Should Know _____

5.   Topic: using lottery to fund public education   Audience: church pastor

Audience Interest _____

Audience Knowledge _____

Audience Vocabulary _____

Audience Should Know _____

6.   Topic: using lottery to fund public education   Audience: governor of state

Audience Interest _____

Audience Knowledge _____

Audience Vocabulary _____

Audience Should Know _____

          Copyright © American Book Company

LANGUAGE AND TONE

Language refers to the words a writer uses. **Tone** is the way the writer uses those words to convey a certain attitude or feeling to the reader. Language (what is said) and tone (how it is said) are determined by the author's purpose and the intended audience. For example, the way you ask someone for a favor is very different from the way you tell someone to leave you alone. Also, the language and tone you use with your friends at the lunch table probably would not be appropriate in the principal's office. To see how language and tone can differ in respect to the audience, read and compare the letter below with the e-mail that follows.

May 17, 2007

Purrfect Pets
621 Peachtree Terrace
Atlanta, Georgia

Dear Sir:

Because of my great love for animals, I am very interested in working at Purrfect Pets. I visit your store frequently as I purchase food and supplies to care for my several cats and dogs. I am always impressed by the cleanliness of your store and the care you show the animals.

This summer I will be available to work full-time. Once school begins in the fall, I will need to reduce my hours to part-time, but I will still be available to work on nights and weekends.

Please find enclosed my application and a list of references. I look forward to hearing from you soon.

Sincerely,

Shauna H. Jones

Shauna H. Jones

Dear Jack,

What's up?! I'm really psyched about workin' at the CD Emporium with you this summer. I mean I don't have the job yet, but why wouldn't they hire me? By the way, can you stop by the CDE on your way to school tomorrow and pick up a job application for me? Thanks! You're the best!

Does your sister still want to work at that stupid pet store? That would gross me out! Cleaning out all those cages with all the animal stuff in it. No thanks! Give me some cellophane-wrapped CDs any day. Catch you later. Thanks again.

T.J.

Copyright © American Book Company

Do you see the similarities and differences between the two letters? Both writers are seeking jobs for the summer, and they want to work where they will enjoy what they will be doing. The authors share a similar purpose, but their audiences are different.

Sally is writing to the owner of the pet shop where she wants to work. She has chosen the language of a business letter to address her potential employer. She avoids dialect and slang terms, and her tone is formal and respectful. The language and tone of T.J.'s e-mail, however, is very different because he is writing to a good friend and is asking a favor. Along with an informal tone, he uses slang terms and abbreviations that Jack will understand easily. Assuming that Jack will recognize T. J.'s style of language, T.J. uses neither his full name nor a salutation such as "sincerely" or "your friend."

The type of language and tone you use in writing greatly affects how the reader will interpret your ideas. This is especially important to consider in persuasive writing. Study the following types and examples of language and tone to help improve your reading and writing.

Different Types of Language

Slang is very informal language that enjoys a brief popularity and then generally becomes obsolete. It is often confined to a limited group of people. **Examples:** crib, dis, groovy, cool, cut it out, word, peace, my bad, etc.

Colloquial English refers to words that are appropriate in dialogue and informal writing but inappropriate in formal writing. Contractions, short words, and clichés may be used. **Examples:** You bet I'll be there! He's in so deep there's no way out! The apple never falls far from the tree.

Non-Standard English contains grammar and usage that do not follow the standard rules for English. The pronouns or verbs are nonstandard.

Standard American English is the English that is most widely accepted in the United States. The grammar used in Standard American English becomes the model for all to follow.

Examples of Non-Standard and Standard English

Non-Standard	Standard
I'm doin' pretty good.	I am well.
I ain't got no money.	I don't have any money.
You and me talks all the time.	You and I talk all the time.

Copyright © American Book Company

Different Types of Tone

angry	stiff	dramatic	optimistic	sad
anxious	relaxed	fearful	pessimistic	tragic
rude	hysterical	happy	formal	humorous
calm	expectant	lofty	informal	serious

Examples of Informal and Formal Tone

Informal	Formal
I'm so psyched!	I am very happy.
How much are you gonna sell that car for?	I wanted to inquire about the car for sale.
Ain't no way I'm gonna work for you.	I regret to say that I must decline your offer of employment.

The Georgia High School Writing Test will ask you to address a particular audience, such as the school principal, other students, or parents. In this case, you should vary your language and tone appropriately. Also, remember that your audience is not your teacher, but a professional reader who has been trained to grade your essay. Therefore, you should strive to use a more formal tone than you would with your teacher. You should also use Standard American English, avoiding slang, colloquial expressions, or non-standard English.

Strive for a more formal tone on the Georgia High School Writing Test, and use Standard American English. Avoid slang, colloquial expressions, and non-standard English.

PRACTICE 4: LANGUAGE AND TONE

Using the terms you have just learned, describe the language and tone you would use in writing to each of the following audiences.

1. **School principal**   Tone _____

    Language _____

2. **Other students**   Tone _____

    Language _____

3. **Good friend**   Tone _____

    Language _____

4. **Editor of the local newspaper**   Tone _____

    Language _____

5. **Manager at work**   Tone _____

    Language _____

PRACTICE 5: LANGUAGE AND TONE

You are running as a representative for your class on the student council. You want to write a short announcement to your friends and to your principal that explains why you are running for this office. How would your language and tone differ for these two audiences? Explain your answer. Then, write a short announcement for each audience.

USING PERSUASIVE LANGUAGE

When you are trying to persuade, you need to present information in a particular way in order to make the reader agree with your position. You must emphasize points of interest to the reader and describe them in language that is attractive to your audience. For example, let's say you worked in a restaurant last year, and you are applying for a new job. When the manager asks what you did at your last job, you could answer with either of the sentences below.

Example 1:   *I mopped floors for a while, and then I took orders at the counter.*

Example 2:   *After proving my abilities by maintaining the restaurant's cleanliness, I was promoted to sales associate.*

    Both sentences provide the same truthful information. However, the second makes you sound like a responsible and hard-working employee, while the first isn't very impressive. If you want to impress your future employer and convince the manager to hire you, the second sentence would be a better choice.

Special Note: Paying attention to your audience does not mean telling people what you think they want to hear or giving false information. Make up your own mind, stay firm, and tell the truth. However, when you present your argument, you want your audience to be able to understand and appreciate what you are saying. So, use words, phrases, and reasons that will persuade your particular audience.

> ***Use words, phrases, and reasons that your audience will understand and appreciate.***

Copyright © American Book Company

PRACTICE 6: PERSUASIVE LANGUAGE

For each of the following situations, write two or three sentences that will influence or persuade the intended reader. The example provided is NOT persuasive.

1. Convince your mother to let your friend sleep over.
   Example: Mom, can Chris please stay tonight?

2. Motivate your team to win.
   Example: It's half-time and we're down by five points. We can win.

3. You took care of your sick brother last night, so you couldn't finish your homework. Persuade your teacher to give you an extension.
   Example: Is it o.k. if I turn in my homework tomorrow?

4. While mowing your neighbors' lawn, you ran over their flower bed. Convince them to give you another chance.
   Example: I think your flowers will grow back before I mow the lawn next time.

PRACTICE 7: PERSUASIVE LANGUAGE

A. Look through newspapers and magazines. Find three examples of persuasive language and determine the author's purpose. Then, find three examples in which the language is not persuasive, and rewrite them in order to persuade the reader to take a stand on one side of the issue. *Hint:* Advertisements and newspaper editorials often contain persuasive language.

B. Imagine that you are the salesperson in the picture to the left. Write four to six sentences to persuade the man behind the desk that a laptop computer will make his work easier and more productive.

C. Imagine that you are president of the junior class. Write four to six sentences that would persuade juniors who drive to school that car pooling is a good idea.

Copyright © American Book Company

BUILDING AN ARGUMENT

Your ability to persuade depends not just on *how* you say something, but also on *what* you have to say. You must be able to build a strong **argument**. In everyday speaking, an "argument" is a disagreement between family members, friends, or enemies who exchange heated words. However, in the context of persuasive writing, an argument is a careful, reasoned way of presenting a point of view. The three steps to building an argument are to **make a claim**, to **support the claim**, and to **answer objections**. This process may be compared to building a pyramid.

Make A Claim

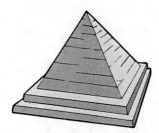

The first step in building a good argument is to **make a claim**. A claim is the position you take on a particular issue. It can't be just a statement of fact. A fact stands alone, cannot be argued, and requires no support. A claim, however, argues for one side of a controversy. Someone may disagree with your claim, so you must support it, just like the pyramid builder needs to support the top of the pyramid. The claim is the "point" you are trying to make, so keep it focused.

Read the following six statements, and decide which are claims that provide a good starting point for an argument.

1. According to a 1999 Harris poll for the National Consumers League, a majority of Americans believe that water is our second-most-threatened resource, after air.
   – Sarah Milstein

2. Through personal choices, economic reform, and improved schools, we, the citizens of this great democracy, must stop the irreversible destruction of our most precious resources: air, water, and children.

3. We ought to be increasing programs that help the hungry children in our country rather than giving more money to an already well-financed program like the military.

4. The effectiveness of closed-circuit cameras in deterring crime in Britain's cities suggests that this strategy would be useful in the United States as well.

5. The best, indeed the only, method of promoting individual and public health is to teach people the laws of nature and thus teach them how to preserve their health.
   – Dr. Herbert Shelton

6. Over the past three decades, there has been increasing public interest in personal self-help books, including the maintenance of health through self-regulated programs of exercise and diet.

Copyright © American Book Company

Statements 1 and 6 present information in a factual, non-persuasive way. The information presented could be used to persuade, but neither statement encourages one belief over another. Statements 2, 3, 4, and 5 urge the reader to take a certain action or have a certain belief. In other words, they make a claim. These statements use words like *must*, *should*, *ought*, *demand*, *only*, and *best*. These key words often indicate that the author is taking a position and encouraging the reader to do the same. You may also notice that the persuasive statements sometimes use the subject *we* in an attempt to involve the reader in the position or idea.

Statement 2 requires a special note. It makes a claim that requires support, but the claim is not focused. Air, water, and children are, indeed, precious resources. However, protecting the environment and improving schools are two topics that would be better addressed by two separate arguments. Try to pick one side of one issue and take a stand. Make sure your "pyramid" has a focused point.

PRACTICE 8: MAKING A CLAIM

For each topic, write a statement of fact and a claim statement. Make it clear that they are different types of statements.

1. Topic: placing parental advisory stickers on music CDs

   Fact: *There is a great deal of controversy over placing parental advisory stickers on music CDs.*

   Claim: *Record companies should not place Parental Advisory stickers on music Cds.*

2. Topic: a year-round school calendar

   Fact: _____

   _____

   Claim: _____

   _____

3. Topic: high salaries of professional athletes

   Fact: _____

   _____

   Claim: _____

   _____

Copyright © American Book Company

4. Topic: lottery funding of education

Fact:_____

_____

Claim: _____

_____

5. Topic: protecting wildlife from construction of new houses on forest land

Fact: _____

_____

Claim: _____

_____

Support The Claim

The entire structure of a pyramid comes to a focused point at the top. Each and every block of the pyramid supports this point. In a similar way, you want each and every sentence of your argument to support your claim. You also want to support your argument with "solid blocks," so it will stand. A strong argument is supported by good logic, solid evidence, and appropriate reasons or examples. A weak argument suffers from poor logic, weak evidence, and faulty reasons or examples. Like a pyramid, a strong argument will stand the test of time.

Read the following two passages about weight loss, and decide whether the arguments are strong or weak.

Rapidly Burn Off Pounds And Inches With SUPER DIET PILL

You Can Lose 10, 20, 50, Even 100 Pounds!
  This is it! This is the diet pill researchers around the world have hailed for its powerful, quick-working ingredients that help people shed stubborn fat–fast!

Super Diet Pill Satisfies Need For Fast Action Without Strenuous Dieting
  So fast-working, you can see a dramatic difference in just two days, without complicated calorie counting or suffering from biting hunger pains. Even people with long-time weight problems find they can burn off up to a pound of fat and fluid every five hours.

50% Fat Loss In 14 To 21 Days
  The longer you use the pill, the more weight you lose. You don't have to stop until you reach the weight that *you* want. Without making major sacrifices or drastic changes, you can shed as much as 50% of your fat in just 2 or 3 weeks.

Copyright © American Book Company

Increased Metabolism Means Weight Loss

One-half of the women and one-fourth of the men in the United States are trying to lose weight and become fit. The sad truth is that most of us will regain our original weight in a year or less. What's the real secret for losing weight and keeping it off?

The answer is developing and maintaining a healthy metabolism. Metabolism refers to how the body burns energy. A person with a high metabolism burns more calories than a person with a low metabolism. Consequently, the person who burns more calories has an easier time losing weight. Here are some tips for improving your metabolism and melting away that extra fat:

1) **Drink plenty of water.** Filling up on water decreases the appetite. Three quarts of water each day are ideal.
2) **Don't skip meals, especially breakfast.** Eat small meals every two to three hours. In this way, carbohydrates and protein will not be converted into fat.
3) **Eat fat-burning foods.** Raw vegetables, whole grains, fruits, and legumes are your best choices. Consume fruits between meals for extra energy. This healthy snack won't be converted to fat.
4) **Exercise regularly.** Aerobic exercises like swimming, running, and walking are best. Also try lifting weights–a good muscle builder and fat burner. Exercise before you eat. It will decrease your appetite and increase your metabolism.

Each passage strongly suggests a way to lose weight and provides reasons to support its method of weight reduction. Which one is based on valid reasons, and which one is based on fallacies?

There are two big clues that the diet pill advertisement is based on fallacies: 1) It sounds too good to be true; and 2) It's trying to sell you something. A good rule of thumb is that if it sounds too good to be true, *it is*, and if someone is trying to sell you something, *beware*. Beyond these initial clues, an examination of the evidence shows that the diet pill ad offers very limited information about the diet pill. Little proof is presented to support its dramatic claims. The ad never mentions the names of the diet pill researchers, the people who lost weight, nor where or when the testing was done.

The description of metabolism, however, bases its argument on biological principles that are common knowledge to most people who have taken a biology class. From this basis, it provides logical explanations of how to increase your body's metabolism. The author is not selling anything and is not offering an easy "quick fix." A decision to follow the suggestions for changes in diet would be based on much better information than a choice to try the diet pill.

Copyright © American Book Company

Three Ways to Build a Strong Argument

1. **Use clear logic and valid facts.** Show cause-effect connections between your position and the reasons you use to support it. Avoid fallacies and use commonly-known, verifiable facts.

2. **Use personal examples that can be generalized.** Although each person's experience is different, events from your life can influence people who face similar situations.

3. **Use statistics or expert testimony.** Despite the fact that statistics can often be misleading, an argument is strengthened by quoting relevant statistics from reliable sources. Expert testimony can also be helpful, as long as the testimony is from a true expert.

"Increased Metabolism Means Weight Loss" is a good example of how to use clear logic and commonly-known facts to build a strong argument. The first story below, "Fire Escape," shows how personal experience can be used to prove a point. The second passage, "Where Are All the Animals?" makes good use of statistics from two different respectable sources. Quoting different sources broadens the base of the argument, making the "pyramid" stronger.

Fire Escape

It may not be fun or even convenient, but every family should develop a fire escape plan and practice it regularly. I never believed this until our fire drills saved our family.

I was so mad when my mom came home from work and announced that we all had to develop and practice a fire escape plan. We had to go outside as quickly as possible from whatever room we were in when Mom rang the bell. My job was to grab my little brother Josh. We had to meet under the maple tree outside our house. Since there were eleven of us, Mom assigned us numbers in case she would forget our names. I hated practicing these fire drills because we had to do these drills in school, too.

One day after two years of these monthly drills, my sister, Carolyn, was playing with logs in the fireplace. Sparks jumped out of the fire and started burning up the living room carpet. Eagerly, the flames licked the furniture and the wallpaper. Smoke filled all of the rooms, setting off our twelve smoke detectors. It was our familiarity with the escape plan that saved our lives, valuables, and even our pets, Fluffy and Foofoo. Unlike our neighbors who had lost all of their valuables in a fire, we were able to save many important pictures and jewelry that had been in our family for decades. After this bad experience, I was very glad we had practiced our fire escape plan.

Copyright © American Book Company

Where Are All the Animals?

Many people believe that Mother Nature can just take care of herself, but in reality, biodiversity, the variety of life forms on Earth, is in trouble. Worldwide, approximately 34% of fish, 25% of mammals, 11% of birds, 20% of reptiles, and 25% of amphibians are on the World Conservation Union (IUCN) Red List of species threatened with extinction. "Currently, we are driving species extinction up to 1000 times faster than the natural rate, which is one in a million per year," says Stuart Pimm, Ph.D., professor of conservation biology at Columbia University in New York. These alarming statistics show how important it is for concerned citizens to support legislation such as the United States Endangered Species Act.

PRACTICE 9: SUPPORTING A CLAIM

Choose three topics from Practice 8: Making a Claim, and choose an audience for each topic. Then, write two ideas you would use to support the claim statement you wrote for Practice 8: Making a Claim.

1. Topic: _parental advisory on CDs_   Audience: _parents_

   Support: a. _Record companies and parents probably have different standards._

   b. _After listening to the music, parents can discuss it with children._

2. Topic: _____   Audience: _____

   Support: a. _____

   b. _____

3. Topic: _____   Audience: _____

   Support: a. _____

   b. _____

4. Topic: _____   Audience: _____

   Support: a. _____

   b. _____

Copyright © American Book Company

Answer Objections

Knowing your audience not only helps you choose an appropriate language and tone, but it also helps you anticipate objections to your position that your audience may have. Answering these possible objections is like building a wall around your pyramid to protect it from anyone who may want to tear it down.

Read the following passage regarding capital punishment, and decide which objections the author is trying to answer.

No More Executions

I want to applaud the governor of Illinois for his recent decision to stop all executions in his state until further review of the capital punishment system. Contrary to popular belief, capital punishment is not a deterrent to crime. In fact, statistics show that states without capital punishment had a lower rate of violent crime in 1999: 3.6 murders per 100,000 persons. States with capital punishment had a higher rate of violent crime in 1999: 5.5 murders per 100,000 persons. Some people claim that the appeals process takes too long, and that's why the death penalty is not a deterrent. However, the Death Penalty Information Center reports that 21 condemned inmates have been released from death row since 1993. This includes seven from the state of Illinois. We cannot risk the execution of innocent people by speeding up the appeals process. The lengthy appeals process also makes capital punishment very expensive. Anyone who has been in a court case knows how much lawyers cost. Those who do not want tax money wasted on criminals should oppose capital punishment because it is actually more expensive to execute someone than to imprison him or her for life. Overall, the system is terribly flawed. The other 38 states with capital punishment laws should join Illinois in placing a moratorium on all executions.

The author of this passage opposes capital punishment and wants to convince others to oppose it as well. In doing so, the writer addresses three popular reasons for supporting the death penalty:

1. capital punishment deters crime;

2. capital punishment would be a deterrent if the appeals process were shorter; and

3. execution is less expensive than life imprisonment.

The author answers these objections to her argument with statistics, authoritative information, and common sense.

> *The three steps to building an argument are to make a claim, to support the claim, and to answer objections.*

Copyright © American Book Company

PRACTICE 10: ANSWERING OBJECTIONS

Return to Practice 9: Supporting a Claim. For each topic you chose, list possible objections to your claim.

1. *1) The stickers prevent parents and children from listening to obviously objectionable music. 2) Parents don't have time to listen to all the music of all their children.*

2. _____

   _____

   _____

3. _____

   _____

   _____

4. _____

   _____

   _____

PRACTICE 11: WRITING PERSUASIVE PARAGRAPHS

Write a persuasive paragraph for each of the three topics you have been working with in Practices 9 and 10. Here's an example:

Parents should not rely on record companies to decide what music their children should or should not buy. Each parent has different standards for what kind of music is appropriate for his or her children. Some people say that parental advisory stickers will "weed-out" the really rude music. However, couldn't this also lull parents into a false sense of security, tempting them to rely only on the record companies? When parents listen to what their children are hearing, they can then discuss the music with their children. If parents don't think they have time for this, then they should re-examine their priorities. Parents have the responsibility for raising their own children. They can't let the record companies do it.

Copyright © American Book Company

CHAPTER 2 SUMMARY: WRITING TO PERSUADE

- *Your purpose for the Georgia High School Writing Test is to persuade.*

- *Your audience for the Georgia High School Writing Test may be parents, students, or local officials, but professional readers will grade your essay.*

- *Strive for a more formal tone on the Georgia High School Writing Test, and use Standard American English. Avoid slang, colloquial expressions, and non-standard English.*

- *Use words, phrases, and reasons that your audience will understand and appreciate.*

- *The three steps to building an argument are to make a claim, to support the claim, and to answer objections.*

Copyright © American Book Company

CHAPTER 2 REVIEW: WRITING TO PERSUADE

Read the following two reports. Then answer the questions below, using complete sentences.

Report 1

The County Government meeting broke up after a long debate. Daryl Smith's supporters claim that he is the duly elected representative of the people and should be allowed to take his seat on the council. His opponents disputed this, saying that his previous protests of council activities disqualify him from holding public office.

Report 2

We elected Daryl Smith, and he's our man. His enemies are just jealous. They think they can throw some mud around and make it stick to Daryl. No way! He's squeaky clean. There ain't nothin' they can do to make him look bad. He stood up for us before, makin' sure the council listened to us. Now those jokers say that's a bad thing. Stick by Daryl. He stuck by us!

1. What is the author's purpose in each report?

2. Compare and contrast the language and tone of these two reports.

Read the following excerpt, and complete the writing exercise that follows.

I stand as firm as the rock of Gibraltar on the right that women have to shape the thoughts, socially and politically, of the world. They can make our country better and purer, just as they appreciate their own rights. I am in favor of women's rights–in their rights to rise up in the majesty of the nature their Creator gave them and emancipate themselves from the foolish fashions and sentiments of the age. When they do rise, they will be more respected by all mankind than all the rulers of the earth from Adam down to the present day.

– Clarissa's speech in *Shams* by John S. Draper

3. Write one paragraph in which you evaluate the language and tone of this excerpt. What are some strengths of the author's choices in language and tone, and what are some weaknesses? How do these affect the persuasiveness of the writing?

Read the following excerpt, and complete the writing exercise on the next page.

There is still a great deal of controversy about the future of the space program. While some people believe it is a waste of much needed funds, others point to the great scientific and technological advances that have resulted from the exploration of space. Supporters of the program most frequently cite the wide uses of microprocessors as one of the major contributions to space-related research. Opponents believe the billions of dollars dedicated to the space program would be better spent on the needs of education, health care, and job training for the poor and disadvantaged.

4. Pick one side of the controversy described above, and write a paragraph to persuade another student of your point of view. Share your paragraph with your classmates. Ask for feedback that would strengthen your argument, and incorporate it into your paragraph. Then, write a letter to the President of the United States expressing your opinion. Show the letter to your teacher. Then, address the letter to The White House, 1600 Pennsylvania Avenue, Washington, D.C. 20500, and send it in the mail.

Read the following two letters which nominate Mr. Jimenez for Teacher of the Year. Then, complete the writing exercise that follows.

Dear Fellow Students,

   I am nominating Mr. Jimenez for Teacher of the Year, and you should, too. Whether you've been in this school for 1 or 4 years, you know he's got a reputation for being tough. But, he's also known for spending hours after school with kids who need help. (And most of us need help to pass his class.)
   You also know how much work he put into the school fair last fall. What a blast that was! Remember how shocked we all were to find out <u>he</u> was the clown?! This is only one way he has shown his love for this school and its students.
   Think of how great it would be to hear the announcement that the Teacher of the Year is from Eastside. People across the state would see what a great school we are. So, when the nominating paper comes around, sign it, and show Mr. Jimenez your support.

Thanks,
Bill Johnson

Dear Members of the School Board,

   I am writing to nominate Mr. Victor P. Jimenez for Teacher of the Year. As the chair of the Biology Department at Eastside High School, he has challenged his students with a rigorous curriculum and demanding standards of excellence. At the same time, he has shown true devotion as an educator by helping students meet those standards through after school tutoring.
   Mr. Jimenez is not only dedicated to academic excellence but also to the development of the school community. Just one example of this is the after school hours he spent in organizing our school's Fall Fair. During this successful event, Mr. Jimenez showed his sense of humor and surprised us all by dressing up like a clown.
   The Teacher of the Year award will honor not only Mr. Jimenez and Eastside High School, but it will honor the State School Board by showing the high educational standards set by this state. Mr. Jimenez provides an example of academic rigor coupled with school spirit that has been an inspiration to our school. He well deserves the title of "Teacher of the Year."

Sincerely,
William H. Johnson

5. The same student wrote the above letters about the same topic for the same purpose. However, each letter is addressed to a different audience. Write a paragraph which describes how these two letters differ because of audience. Be sure to discuss language and tone as well as audience knowledge, interest, and vocabulary.

Copyright © American Book Company

Read the following two letters about trash pick-up, and answer the questions that follow.

To the editor:

This is America! Some people want to decide for me who's going to take my trash away. They say there are too many trash trucks in this neighborhood. Well, my son owns a trash company that services this neighborhood, and he says there're only a few other companies that he competes with, and he should know.

Each resident in this city has the right and the responsibility to choose the trash company that he or she wants. Whichever company provides the best service for the needs of its customers should get the most business. Only in a Communist state could it be legal for groups of citizens to band together and limit free choices of consumers and businesses alike. Where would such limitation end? Maybe the different churches shouldn't have their services on the same day because it causes too many cars to drive through the neighborhood.

I whole-heartedly oppose any attempt by the neighborhood association to regulate which company can pick up my family's trash and on what day they can do it. I've been living in this neighborhood for 45 years, and I've never heard of such a ridiculous idea. And, if the neighborhood association tries to pull off such an unfounded scheme, they will find themselves in court!

Your fellow citizen,

Joan Zemsy

Joan Zemsy

To the editor:

Lately, our neighborhood has seemed like a cross between Grand Central Station and the city dump. In the process of gathering information to present to the neighborhood association, I sat by my window and counted the number of garbage trucks that passed in one week: Eleven! An incredible number? I surveyed twenty residents in our neighborhood and found that, in fact, twelve different trash companies are contracted.

I am certainly in support of free enterprise; I believe that freedom of commerce is one of the things that makes America great. However, I also believe in peace and quiet, proper sanitation, and the safety of my children.

I guess I'm lucky that only eleven trucks pass by my house instead of the twelve that could possibly rumble past my door, shaking my windows and rattling my teeth. A trash truck is a huge vehicle which makes a lot of noise when the massive hydraulic compactor goes into action. Once per week this inconvenience may be tolerable, but not two or three times per day.

These trucks also spit out a lot of foul smells and black smoke into the neighborhood. And what about the safety of our children? Should they have to dodge piles of garbage that line our sidewalks every day of the week? And when they ride their bikes to a friend's house, should they fear that from around each corner could come a thundering garbage truck?

Simple common sense demands that all residents of our neighborhood band togther to hire one trash company to come once per week to take away our trash.

Sincerely,

Jamal Waterford

Jamal Waterford

6. How do the language and tone differ in the two letters?

7. Which letter is more persuasive? Why? Explain your answer.

ADDITIONAL ACTIVITIES: WRITING TO PERSUADE

1. In Practice 11 of this chapter, you wrote three different paragraphs on three different topics. Now, write three more paragraphs on the same topics, but each for a different audience. You will want to vary your language and tone, answer different possible objections, and use different support. Return to Practice Exercises 3, 8, 9, and 10 to help you develop your paragraphs.

    The paragraph below is an example of writing to other students about Parental Advisory stickers. Compare this paragraph with the one on page 55.

    Record companies should not place Parental Advisory stickers on music CD's. The record industry wants us to believe it's helping unknowing consumers. As teenagers, we know what is on a CD before we buy it. We hear songs on the radio, talk to friends, watch MTV, and decide what music we want to purchase. If a CD has controversial lyrics we know it, and we know what our parents will not allow. All the music industry is doing is creating controversy and hype over bad music. Some people say the stickers help parents. Well, all parents are different, and they need to listen to the music themselves. Parental Advisory stickers create more sales because of publicity. However, they are not much help to parents and should be removed.

2. Develop three persuasive paragraphs on the same topic but for three different audiences, such as high school students, teachers, your principal, parents, members of the local school board, readers of the local newspaper, or the programming director of a television station. Here are some possible topics with which you can agree or disagree.

    raising the driving age to 18   **offensive bumper stickers**
    voting on the Internet   **sex before marriage**
    using cell phones while driving   **praying in school**
    no homework policy for high school students   **race prejudice in school**

3. Make a list of 3-4 movies or videos you have seen recently. Choose one of them, and write a one-paragraph review in which you persuade your readers why they should or should not see the movie.

4. A new student is attending his first day of class in your school. In one paragraph, advise him or her on how to survive/succeed in your school.

5. Several girls in your high school want to play on the football team. In one paragraph, convince the coach, the principal, or the school board why these girls should or should not play on the football team.

6. While you were washing your hands in the rest room of the locker room, you saw your best friend sneak into the locker room and steal money from the pants pockets of students who were out in gym class. In one paragraph, persuade your friend to confess the crime and accept the consequences.

Copyright © American Book Company

Chapter 3
Planning the Essay

After practicing writing persuasive paragraphs, you are ready to focus specifically on mastering the Georgia High School Writing Test. In this chapter, you will learn about the following:

- **The Basic Structure of an Essay**
- **The Writing Process**
- **Generating Ideas**
- **Focusing Ideas**
- **Making a Plan for Your Essay**

BASIC STRUCTURE OF AN ESSAY

The essay you will create for the Georgia High School Writing Test should include three main parts: the **introduction**, the **body**, and the **conclusion**.

Basic Structure of an Essay

> **INTRODUCTION**
> 1 Paragraph:
> General Discussion
> & Statement of
> Controlling Idea

↓

> **BODY**
> 1-3 Paragraphs:
> Elaboration of
> Controlling Idea with
> Supporting Details

↓

> **CONCLUSION**
> 1 Paragraph:
> Summary of Discussion

The **introduction** is the first paragraph of your essay. It gets the reader's attention, prepares the reader for what will follow, and states the **controlling idea** of the essay. The controlling idea of an essay is much like the main idea of a paragraph.

The **body** consists of one to three paragraphs which support the controlling idea. Each paragraph is focused around a topic sentence which can be drawn from the key points of the controlling idea. In turn, the topic sentence of each paragraph is supported by the details explained in the rest of that paragraph.

Copyright © American Book Company

The **conclusion** is the last paragraph of your essay. It reinforces the controlling idea of your essay with a vigorous summary of your argument. It ties everything together and convinces the reader of the rightness of your position.

THE WRITING PROCESS

The essay you compose for the Georgia High School Writing Test is like any other writing you do in that it does not appear magically. You must follow a process. You have to **think**, **write**, **review**, and then repeat these steps. Study the writing process described below.

The Writing Process

THINK

1. **Read the Writing Prompt Carefully.** Make sure that you understand what question the writing prompt is asking and who your audience is.

2. **Generate Ideas.** Make a list of every idea that comes into your head regarding the topic. Don't judge the ideas as good or bad yet.

3. **Focus Your Ideas.** From your list, choose some ideas that you can use for your essay, and make a plan for how you will present them.

WRITE

4. **Write.** Write a draft based on your plan. Use complete sentences to develop your ideas into paragraphs.

REVIEW

5. **Revise.** Check over your draft for coherence, transitions, and sentence variety and structure. Delete any unnecessary words, phrases, or sentences.

THINK

6. **Think** about any other ways you can improve your essay.

WRITE

7. **Write** the final copy of your essay clearly on the lined paper.

REVIEW

8. **Proofread.** Neatly correct punctuation, spelling, capitalization, word choice, grammar, and sentence formation.

It may seem like there are many steps to follow when you only have a limited amount of time to write an essay. For now, go through the steps slowly, learning each one thoroughly. As you practice, these steps will become like second nature to you. Then, you will be well prepared for the Georgia High School Writing Test.

> *Practice the writing process: think, write, and review.*

Copyright © American Book Company

READ THE WRITING PROMPT CAREFULLY

The first step in writing a good response is to read the writing prompt carefully. Make sure you understand the **question** you are to answer. It is also important for you to identify the **audience** to whom you are writing, such as the principal, other students, or readers of the local newspaper. Read the following sample writing prompt carefully.

Writing Situation

    A recent survey has shown that teens aged 12 to 17 watch an average of eleven hours of television each week. However, children between the ages of 2 and 5 watch an average of thirteen hours of television each week. Your teacher has given you the homework assignment: discuss with your family the amount of television watched in your home. Decide what you think about young children watching nearly two hours of television each day.

Directions for Writing

    As a way of introducing the topic of children watching television, you will write an essay answering the following question: "Does television affect young children positively or negatively? Explain your answer." Once you finish the essay, you will give it to your parents to "look over." This will start your family's discussion.

---

1.   What question does this writing prompt ask?   ⟶   "Does television affect young children positively or negatively?"

The writing prompt does not ask you to address whether your family watches too much television, or why teens watch less television than younger children. The prompt asks whether television affects young children positively or negatively. Stick to this issue.

Watching television may affect young children in both positive and negative ways. You must decide if, overall, the effects are positive *or* negative. **For persuasive writing, it is important to choose one side of an issue.** Though it is helpful for you to acknowledge and/or answer possible objections to your position, do not try to argue both sides of the issue at the same time. Since your purpose is to persuade the reader, you must first be clear about your own position.

2.   Who is the audience?   ⟶   Your parents

    Of course, the teacher will be reading this sample essay, but you will also share it with your parents. This dilemma of a dual audience is similar to the Georgia High School Writing Test in that you will be asked to address a certain audience, but the essay will be graded by professional readers. In response to this sample writing prompt, you must use more formal language and tone for your teacher, while at the same time being aware of comments or objections your parents may have.

Answer the correct question for the proper audience.

GENERATING IDEAS

Once you clearly understand what the writing prompt is asking, you can begin generating ideas to use in your response. You may have many good ideas, but they aren't useful until you get them out of your head onto the paper. **Brainstorming** and **freewriting** are two methods of getting your ideas out of your head, so you can work with them.

Brainstorming

One way to explore possibilities for your essay is through **brainstorming**. Begin writing down whatever comes to mind regarding the topic and questions provided by the writing prompt. Do not worry about grammar or spelling, and don't make any decisions about the ideas as you write them. Just let them flow freely from your thoughts. Your purpose is to create a list of ideas and details that you can use to develop your essay. For example, a brainstorming list based on the prompt on the previous page could look something like this:

What's wrong with television?
learn new information
kids are quiet
kids need exercise
they should be out playing
safe places to play?
educational programs
Barney, Sesame Street, NYPD Blue
see lots of commercials!
sex is used in commercials
kids like TV
Too many hours in front of the tube
tv is violent
sitting around playing video games
what if parents aren't home
kids watch too much TV

As you can see from the list above, the process of brainstorming helps you generate ideas for your essay, but it also can help you clarify your thoughts. As the ideas flowed freely onto the page, the student who wrote the above brainstorming list developed an opinion about the effects of television on young children.

PRACTICE 1: BRAINSTORMING

Create a brainstorming list for each of the following topics:

1. Should prayer be allowed in public schools?

2. What are the effects of having metal detectors at the doors of your school?

3. Agree or disagree with the following statement: "All teenagers should be required to complete a driver's education course before they are approved for a driver's permit."

4. Air pollution is increasing in your area. How should your community respond?

Copyright © American Book Company

Freewriting

Freewriting is another way to write down ideas that you can use for an essay. When some people are asked a question, they just start talking to help them think out loud. Sometimes, this is how people find out what their thoughts are. When you freewrite, you simply start writing and see what happens. Don't worry about grammar and spelling. If you get stuck and don't know what to put next, write "I don't know what to write." Just keep writing, and let the ideas flow. Look at the following freewriting sample about the topic of school uniforms.

> *school uniforms are stupid. I want to wear what I want to wear. Can you see me in one of those silly skirts? Those colors are always so bad. Who woudl want unifiorms anyway? How much do they cost. I couldl never get a date if I were wearing a uniform. I don't know what to write Schoool uniforms stifle student individuality. Everyones an individual we don't need to look the same. What are the benefits. As long as clothing is clean and respectable, why do we all have to wear the same thing? Think of the added expense of buying two sets of clothes. Clothes that can conly be worn at school and closthes t home, I wouldn't be caught dead in one of those schoool uiformns otuside fo school*

Obviously, the student who wrote this has some strong opinions that could lead to a good essay.

> *To generate ideas for your essay, write down whatever you think, without making judgments about it.*

PRACTICE 2: FREEWRITING

Try freewriting about each of the following topics:

1. The need for improved public transportation in your area.

2. Life contains many joyful moments. What was the happiest day of your life?

3. School activities such as field trips, plays, and concerts can be fun and educational. What was your favorite school activity last semester?

4. Cheating in school is the wrong way to get an education. How should students who are caught cheating be punished?

FOCUSING IDEAS

Obviously, you cannot create an essay directly from a brainstorming list or a freewriting sample. The ideas don't follow any logical order. Also, there are too many ideas. You can't use them all. You need to choose a group of related ideas that you can develop into a coherent, well-organized essay. **Clustering** can help you organize your thoughts and develop the **controlling idea** for your essay.

Clustering

Clustering is one helpful way to start organizing your ideas by grouping related thoughts together. In the clustering process, you put the main question of the writing prompt in the center of the page, and draw a circle around it. Then, you draw branches off from this circle to add topics and supporting details.

Sample Clustering for Effects of Television on Young Children

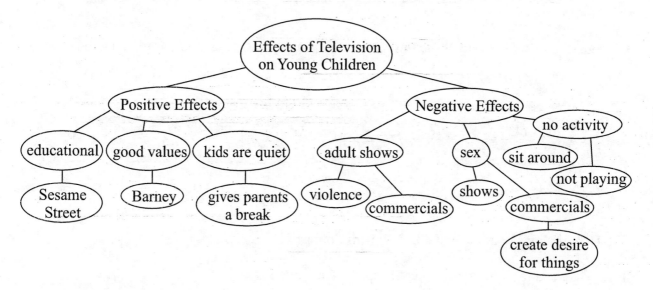

The clustering process can help you narrow your ideas, but these ideas still need to be limited further. You can choose only one portion of your cluster to develop your essay. For example, in the cluster diagram above, there are more ideas grouped around the negative effects of television. This indicates interest, enthusiasm, and support for this idea, and would, therefore, make a good focus for an essay.

PRACTICE 3: CLUSTERING

Choose four of the topics from Practice 1 or Practice 2, and create a clustering diagram for each one. (You will use these diagrams for Practice 5, so keep them in your portfolio.)

Copyright © American Book Company

Controlling Idea

Your response to the writing prompt will be focused around the **controlling idea** of your essay. The controlling idea is the main point–the idea you are trying to prove. It is what *you* want to say. The controlling idea must be broad enough to invite discussion but narrow enough to be manageable in three to five paragraphs. It summarizes the topic and purpose of your essay in one sentence and includes the general topic, your focus, and supporting points. Look at the example below:

General Topic	Focus	Supporting points
Television affects young children	in a negative way	exposing them to adult programs commercials increase desires for things decreases playful activity

A sentence which states the controlling idea would look like this:

Television affects young children negatively by exposing them to adult programs, increasing their desire for needless products, and decreasing their playful activity.

The statement of the controlling idea for your essay is similar to the topic sentence of a paragraph. It provides the reader with valuable information about what is to come, and it gives you a kind of compass to keep your essay on track. As you will see in the next section, you can use each of the supporting points from your controlling idea to form topic sentences for the body paragraphs.

> *Use clustering to help you develop the controlling idea for your essay.*

PRACTICE 4: CONTROLLING IDEA

A. **Below are three topics that have been focused in a specific way. Choose another way to focus each topic, and provide three supporting points.**

	General Topic	Focus	Supporting Points
1.	School uniforms	not good idea	look bad limit individuality more expensive
	School uniforms	*good idea*	*less distracting dress* *promote professional attitude* *large families pass down to younger kids*

General Topic	Focus	Supporting Points
2. Part-time jobs for students	unrewarding and time consuming	decrease study time pay low hourly wages interfere with social life
Part-time jobs for students	_____ _____	_____ _____ _____
3. Driver's education	teens should be required	parents can't teach they feel invincible everyone should be required
Driver's education	_____ _____	_____ _____ _____
4. Metal detectors at school doors	should be installed when principal decides necessary	increases safety in schools invasion of privacy worth it airports do the same thing
Metal detectors at school doors	_____ _____	_____ _____ _____

B. For 2, 3, and 4 above, choose the position you support. Then, write a statement of the controlling idea for three different essays in which you will defend your position.

1. _____

_____

2. _____

_____

3. _____

_____

Copyright © American Book Company

MAKING A PLAN

Your controlling idea is like the destination you have chosen for a journey. The ideas you have gathered in your clustering diagram are the stops you want to make along the way. You still need to decide how you will get to your destination, putting your stops in the proper order. An **outline** helps you plan your journey.

Outline

An **outline** lays out the plan for your essay in a very structured way. It is the road map you will follow in writing your draft. You will get to your destination more easily if your road map looks like the following:

I.   Introduction: General discussion including statement of controlling idea

II. Body

    A.   Paragraph 1: Topic 1 (from statement of controlling idea) and supporting details

    B.   Paragraph 2: Topic 2 (from statement of controlling idea) and supporting details

    C.   Paragraph 3: Topic 3 (from statement of controlling idea) and supporting details

III. Conclusion: Summary of discussion

An outline for the essay about the effects of television on young children might look like this:

I.   Introduction: Television affects young children negatively by exposing them to adult programs, increasing their desire for needless products, and decreasing their playful activity.

II. Body

    A.   Television exposes children to adult programs.

        1.   Theft

        2.   Murder

        3.   Sex

    B.   Commercials increase children's desires for needless products.

        1.   Children find it difficult to distinguish reality from fiction

        2.   Products bring happiness

    C.   Television decreases children's playful activity.

        1.   Lack of interaction with others

        2.   No fresh air and movement

III. Conclusion: Young children should watch less television

Copyright © American Book Company

Outline Shortcut

An outline can be very helpful for organizing an essay when you have a longer time to complete an essay. However, the GHSWT gives you only 100 minutes to compose your response.

One way to save time is to use your clustering diagram to create an **outline shortcut** in place of a complete outline. You can look at the clustering diagram you have already produced, and write "CI" next to the circle that will be your controlling idea. Then, choose two or three circles from which you can form your body paragraphs, and put them in order by writing 1, 2, or 3 next to them. You may even want to group a few ideas for one paragraph by circling them. With this shorthand notation, you have made a kind of outline that will help you write your introduction around the controlling idea and support it with the body paragraphs according to the order you have chosen. Then, you can summarize your key ideas in your conclusion.

See below how the clustering diagram from page 66 can be used in this way.

Sample Outline Shortcut for Effects of Television on Young Children

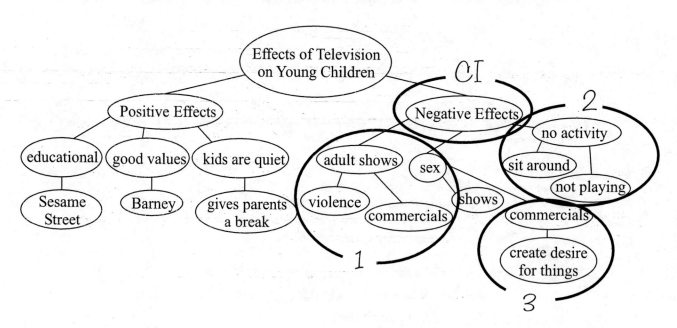

> *Use an outline or your clustering diagram to make a plan for your essay.*

PRACTICE 5: MAKING A PLAN

A. Choose two of the topics for which you have generated ideas, and develop outlines for each one.

B. Choose two of the clustering diagrams you have made, and organize each one into an outline shortcut.

Copyright © American Book Company

CHAPTER 3 SUMMARY: PLANNING THE ESSAY

- **Basic structure of an essay:**

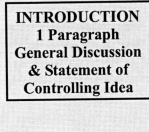

INTRODUCTION
1 Paragraph
General Discussion
& Statement of
Controlling Idea

BODY
1-3 Paragraphs
Elaboration of
Controlling Idea with
Supporting Details

CONCLUSION
1 Paragraph
Summary of Discussion

- **Practice the writing process: *think, write, and review*.**

- **Answer the correct question for the proper audience.**

- **To generate ideas for your essay, write down whatever you think without making judgments about it.**

- **Use clustering to help you develop the controlling idea for your essay.**

- **Use an outline or your clustering diagram to make a plan for your essay.**

Copyright © American Book Company

CHAPTER 3 REVIEW: PLANNING THE ESSAY

Note: Keep your papers from this Chapter Review in your portfolio. You will use the work you have done here in the Reviews for other chapters in this book.

A.   **Read the following writing prompts. On a separate sheet of paper, write the question asked and the intended audience for each prompt. The first exercise has been completed for you.**

Prompt:

> <u>Writing Situation</u>
>
> This year the Parent Teacher Association (PTA) is planning an extended field trip for the junior class. The parents and teachers want to make sure the trip is educational, but they also want it to be entertaining. In order to make a good choice, the PTA is seeking input from the students. What do you think would be a good place for an entertaining and educational field trip?
>
> <u>Directions for Writing</u>
>
> Write a letter to the PTA describing the place you think your class should go for its field trip. Remember that the PTA is interested in education, not just entertainment. Use good reasons and examples to convince the PTA to select the destination that you think is best.

Answer: Question: *What do you think would be a good place for an entertaining and educational field trip?*
Audience: *parents and teachers in the PTA*

1.   <u>Writing Situation</u>

Many students today work while they are in school. While some people cite the heightened sense of responsibility and discipline it brings to students in their academics, others believe the hours spent working interfere with the time needed for studying and doing homework. Is it an advantage or disadvantage to have a job while you are in school?

<u>Directions for Writing</u>

Write an e-mail to post on a student message board in which you argue whether working while in school is an advantage or a disadvantage. Try to convince visitors to the discussion board to agree with you by providing a well-developed argument.

2.   <u>Writing Situation</u>

Many school districts are now considering the idea of school vouchers. In the voucher system, parents who do not want to send their children to public schools will receive a voucher which can be used to pay for tuition at any accredited private school. Is this initiative a good idea or not?

<u>Directions for Writing</u>

Write an e-mail message to be posted on a discussion board for high school students in your area. Include reasons and evidence to convince your peers to support your position.

Copyright © American Book Company

3. <u>Writing Situation</u>

    Your local newspaper is sponsoring a contest with a $10,000 prize. The contestants must write a two-page essay which answers the question, "If you were granted one wish to change the world, what would you change?"

<u>Directions for Writing</u>

    Write a convincing essay for the judges. Describe the one thing you would change in the world. Also, describe why this change would be the best change for the entire world community. Include detailed and convincing information to show that your idea will have the greatest possible positive impact on the world.

4. <u>Writing Situation</u>

    Your parents have informed you that they will be moving to another state during the middle of your senior year in high school. One of your relatives, however, lives in the area of your school. How do you feel about the prospect of moving?

<u>Directions for Writing</u>

    Write a persuasive letter to your parents either convincing them to let you stay on at the high school or persuading them that you would be better off moving with them to another state. Be sure you give appropriate reasons in your letter that would appeal to your parents' ways of thinking.

5. <u>Writing Situation</u>

    You just read in the newspaper that your school district is considering changing the school year schedule to require students to go to school year-round, with a month-long break in December and July. Many students are in an uproar because they enjoy having a long summer vacation to take extended trips. However, many teachers and parents support the proposal because students would remember more information. Decide what you believe concerning this issue.

<u>Directions for Writing</u>

    Write a letter to the superintendent in your school district explaining why you are for or against this proposed change. Be sure you include how the change would affect the lives of students, parents, teachers, and administrators on an educational and a personal level.

Note: If you would rather write about a different topic, choose one of the thirty sample writing prompts in Appendix A (pages 177-184).

B. On a separate sheet of paper, write down your brainstorming ideas about topics 1, 2, and 3 from Part A.

Field Trip Example: *Disney World, Epcot Center, cultural showcases, technology, innovations, Tomorrowland, Living Seas, Disney characters, Magic Kingdom, interactive exhibits, computer simulators, computer software, bumper cars, unlimited video games, custom-designed roller coasters, Space Ship Earth, exhibits, native food and workers, native animals.*

C. On a separate sheet of paper, freewrite your ideas surrounding topics 4 and 5 from Part A.

Field Trip Example: *Members of the PTA, I think we should go to Orlando, Florida, to have our field trip. We would have a great time. I remember going into Disney Quest, we could play video games for free all day. In Epcot, you can tour many important countries of the world and eat their food, too. I remember going to the Magic Kingdom. You see, at night they do this special show called Parade of Lights. It's pretty fun. Of course, they have the Disney characters over there too, Oh yeah, did I forget to mention that Epcot has all of these special attractions where you get to explore and experience some great technological innovations. They seem to have new attractions there every year!*

D. On a separate sheet of paper, take each of the ideas from Part B, and organize them by clustering. From these clusters, notice what is in common, and write down the controlling idea.

Field Trip Example (Taken from brainstorming ideas in Example B):

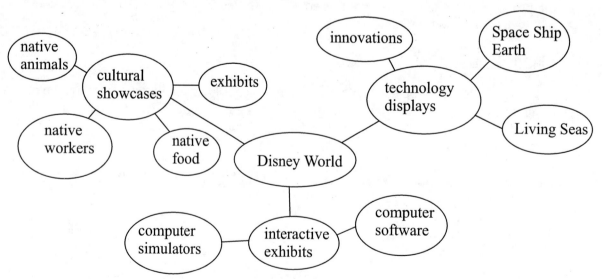

Controlling Idea: *Walt Disney World will provide the best educational and entertainment opportunities because of its cultural showcases, technology displays, and interactive exhibits.*

Copyright © American Book Company

E. Use your clustering diagrams from Part D to create outline shortcuts for topics 1, 2, and 3.

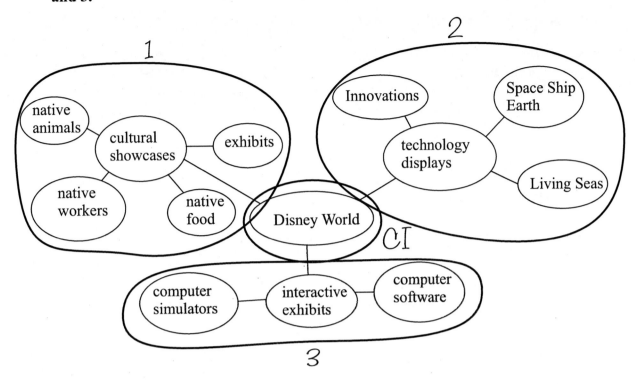

F. On a separate sheet of paper, create an outline for topics 4 and 5 based on the clustering diagrams you designed in Part D.

Example:

    I. Introduction: Walt Disney World will provide the best educational and entertainment opportunities because of its cultural showcases, technology displays, and interactive exhibits.

    II. Body
        A. Cultural showcases
            1. Exhibits and food
            2. Native workers
            3. Native animals
        B. Technology displays
            1. Innovations
            2. Space Ship Earth
            3. Living Seas
        C. Interactive exhibits
            1. Computer simulators
            2. Computer software

    III. Conclusion: Disney World is the best place for this special field trip.

Note: Keep your papers from this Chapter Review in your portfolio. You will use the work you have done here in the Reviews for other chapters in this book.

Copyright © American Book Company

ADDITIONAL ACTIVITIES: PLANNING THE ESSAY

1. As a class, choose one of the following topics to discuss.

    raising the driving age to 18   **offensive bumper stickers**
    voting on the Internet   **year round school**
    using cell phones while driving   **praying in school**
    no homework policy for high school students   **race prejudice in school**
    benefits of studying a foreign language   **your favorite cars**

    Once your class has chosen a topic, each student, individually, should create a brainstorming list of ideas regarding that topic. Then, students should gather in small groups to share, compare, and further develop their lists. The class should then create a large brainstorming list by writing ideas on the chalk board. Finally, the class should choose which ideas would make the strongest essay.

2. Choose another topic from #1. On your own, freewrite on this topic for about 10 minutes. Then, gather in small groups to share, compare, and further develop your freewriting. Finally, as a class, create one extensive freewriting sample on the board or overhead projector. Then, choose the ideas that would make the best essay.

3. In #1, you developed a brainstorming list, and in #2, you created a freewriting sample. Now, choose either one, and develop a clustering diagram. Then discuss your clustering in a small group. Finally, contribute your best ideas to a clustering diagram for the entire class.

4. Review your clustering diagram from #3. Then circle and label the part of your cluster that would be an outline shortcut. Use the sample outline shortcut on page 70 as a guide.

5. Based on your outline shortcut from #3, create a controlling idea for your essay. Write it down, and then compare it with the controlling ideas from other students in the class. Make sure it includes your topic, your focus, and your supporting ideas.

Copyright © American Book Company

Chapter 4
Drafting the Essay

Once you have generated ideas, focused the ideas, and made a plan for your essay, you are ready to start writing a **draft**. A draft is an attempt to put all of your ideas and planning onto paper in the form of an essay. You develop this draft by organizing complete sentences into paragraphs.

Some people like to write several drafts, changing and improving each one significantly. Other people spend more time being precise the first time and may write only two or three drafts. On the Georgia High School Writing Test, you will probably have only enough time to write one draft, revise it, write the final copy, and proofread it. That is why it is important for you to practice writing essays now, so it will be easier for you to do during the writing test.

This chapter will help you prepare for the Georgia High School Writing Test by providing practice in the following areas:

- **Improving Word Choice**
- **Choosing Active Voice**
- **Writing Introductions and Conclusions**
- **Using Transitional Words**
- **Developing Coherence**
- **Writing the Draft**

IMPROVING WORD CHOICE

Your draft is an attempt to convey your ideas accurately and in an interesting way to the reader. Once you have identified your audience and decided which tone and language would be appropriate, you will select certain words and phrases to reflect these decisions. Your **word choice** is an important way to interest the reader, accurately convey your ideas, and persuade the reader to agree with you. Improving word choice involves **selecting specific words, using a dictionary and thesaurus**, **being aware of connotations and denotations**, and **avoiding clichés and sweeping generalizations**.

Select Specific Words, Not General Words

One aspect of good word choice is selecting specific and concrete words rather than general or abstract words. Avoid vague, overused words like *thing*, *nice*, *great*, *bad*, *good*, and *a lot*. These words have many meanings, but none are very clear or specific. Specific words provide the reader with a clear image of what you are describing. For example, compare the two passages below which describe the same event.

Example 1:   *As we rode down away from the hill, the lightning kept flashing and flashing. One thunderclap followed right after another, but each sounded very strange. The lightning made it hard to see, and hail hit the windshield as I continued to drive.*

Example 2: *A moderate incline runs towards the foot of Maybury Hill, and down this we clattered. Once the lightning had begun, it went on in as rapid a succession of flashes as I have ever seen. The thunderclaps, treading one on the heels of another and with a strange crackling accompaniment, sounded more like the working of a gigantic electric machine than the usual detonating reverberations. The flickering light was blinding and confusing, and a thin hail smote gustily at [the windshield] as I drove down the slope.*

– H. G. Wells, *The War of the Worlds*

As you can see from Example 1, general words provide a bland description, while in Example 2, concrete words paint a vivid picture. A good way to improve your word choice is to try to answer the questions *who?*, *what?*, *where?*, *when?*, *why?*, and *how?* in as much detail as you can. Take, for example, the following sentence:

Example 3: *When he hit the home run, the crowd cheered.*

The sentence tells the basic facts, but it could be improved significantly with a more detailed description. Consider the following questions: Who hit the ball? How did he hit it? Where did it go? How did it get there? In what way did the crowd cheer? To answer these questions, one might write the following sentence:

Example 4: *When John's mighty swing sent the ball hurtling over the rightfield fence, the crowd leapt to its feet and burst into wild cheers.*

In this sentence, the writer gives detailed answers to the above questions and provides a vivid picture of what happened. Good descriptions are more interesting and more persuasive.

PRACTICE 1: USING SPECIFIC WORDS

Fill in the blanks with the appropriate words. The first two are completed as examples.

	General	More Specific	Very Specific
1.	athlete	football player	wide receiver
2.	food	fruit	banana
3.	animal	_____	cocker spaniel
4.	_____	pop music	hip-hop
5.	car	S.U.V.	_____
6.	_____	pop-music star	Norah Jones

Copyright © American Book Company

7.	_____	below freezing	12° F
8.	young	school age	_____
9.	tree	_____	pine
10.	government official	_____	President Bush

PRACTICE 2: USING SPECIFIC WORDS

Rewrite the following sentences using specific words to create more vivid descriptions.

1. The dog barked all night long.

2. The strong wind caused a tree to fall on our house.

3. It was so hot, we had to jump into the pool.

4. He almost cried when he saw his son graduate.

5. That book was boring.

Use a Dictionary or Thesaurus

Though you will not be able to use a dictionary or thesaurus on the Georgia High School Writing Test, using them for your practice essays will greatly improve your vocabulary and your writing skills.

When you are unsure of the meaning of a word, look it up. A good **dictionary** will provide you with the most exact meaning of the word. For example, try looking up the words "flammable" and "inflammable." You may be surprised at what you find.

When you can't find just the right word to express the idea or picture you want to convey, go to a **thesaurus**. A thesaurus provides many different words that have similar meanings. For example, if you look up the word "see," you will find many interesting alternatives such as *observe, behold, examine, inspect, stare, notice, scan, spy, catch sight of, survey,* or *contemplate.*

PRACTICE 3: USING A DICTIONARY AND THESAURUS

In a thesaurus, look up these common words: eat, sleep, drink, short, big. For each word, list three similar words. In a dictionary, look up the definitions for each of the words you found in the thesaurus. How are the words similar to and different from each other?

Copyright © American Book Company

Be Aware of Connotations and Denotations

One important part of word choice is knowing the difference between the **denotations** (dictionary meanings) and the **connotations** (emotional associations) of words. For example, the words *slender* and *skinny* both mean "thin." However, if you called a person *slender*, that compliment might get you a date. On the other hand, calling the same person *skinny* might be offensive. In a similar way, the words *determined* and *stubborn* both refer to persistence and an unwillingness to be moved from a particular position. However, *determined* carries a positive connotation, while *stubborn* is usually considered a negative word.

PRACTICE 4: CONNOTATIONS AND DENOTATIONS

Use a dictionary to help you describe the connotations and denotations of the following words:

1. watch, glance, stare
2. walk, stroll, meander
3. run, sprint, scurry

4. shivering, trembling, quaking
5. strong, sturdy, tough

Avoid Clichés and Sweeping Generalizations

Avoid using **clichés** in your writing. These overly familiar expressions include popular phrases such as "busy as a bee" and "to make a long story short." These dull, overused expressions interfere with your message. Simple, straightforward language is often more effective. For example,

Clichés	**Simple Language**
busy as a bee	very active
to make a long story short	to summarize
cute as a button	endearing
stop beating around the bush	get to the point
save it for a rainy day	save it for when you need it

Also, avoid **sweeping generalizations** like the following: "No one ever calls me." Unless used for dramatic effect in a story, words like *always, never, ever, no one, everybody,* and *everywhere* are most often not true and show an overly simple understanding of the topic being discussed. Replace these unrealistic claims with accurate descriptions. For example,

Sweeping Generalization	**Accurate Description**
No one ever calls me.	I rarely get phone calls.
It always rains on my birthday.	It seems like every year it rains on my birthday.
Everybody knows that Atlanta has the best team.	Many people believe Atlanta will win the World Series.

Copyright © American Book Company

PRACTICE 5: CLICHÉS AND SWEEPING GENERALIZATIONS

The passage below expresses strong patriotic feelings, but the writer has weakened the impact of the argument by using sweeping generalizations and worn-out phrases. Rewrite the passage by improving the language used.

The United States has always been the most patriotic country. From the beginning, people worked day after day to do the right thing and make this country free. Everyone knows that the United States is the best place in the world to live. You'll never see the good life until you come to the Land of the Free and the Home of the Brave. Nobody can ever deny that our country is Number One.

PRACTICE 6: WORD CHOICE

On your own or with others, review some of your previous written responses, looking for inappropriate word choices. Revise them, using more effective choices of words. (This is a good opportunity to use a dictionary and a thesaurus.)

> *Improve your word choice by using specific words, using a dictionary and thesaurus, being aware of connotations and denotations, and avoiding clichés and sweeping generalizations.*

CHOOSING ACTIVE VOICE

Voice is a term used to indicate the nature of the action in a sentence. There are two types of voice in a sentence: **active** and **passive**. In the **active voice**, the subject of the sentence **performs** the action. In the **passive voice**, the subject of the sentence **receives** the action. Although there are appropriate times to use passive voice, active voice is usually more effective. Consider the examples below.

Example 1: *The virus on the software made our computer system crash.*

In Example 1, the subject, *virus*, is performing the action of crashing the computer system. Thus, the sentence is written in **active** voice.

Example 2: *Our computer system was disabled by the virus.*

In Example 2, the subject, *computer system*, receives the disabling action of the virus. Therefore, this sentence is written in **passive** voice. Note: The word "by" is a signal that the voice is passive.

In persuasive writing, you shouldn't assume or hope that the reader agrees with you. You want to engage the reader and purposefully convince him or her to agree with your position. Using active voice can help you do that.

> *Use active voice.*

Copyright © American Book Company

PRACTICE 7: USING ACTIVE VOICE

Read the sentences below. After each sentence, write whether the sentence is in active or passive voice. If the sentence is in passive voice, rewrite it in active voice. A sample sentence has been done for you.

Sample: **The medicine was prescribed by the doctor.** *Passive*
The doctor prescribed the medicine.

1. Sally returned the borrowed book to her friend, Robbie.

   _____

2. The hole in the garden was completely filled in with compost by someone.

   _____

3. The apple strudel was carefully prepared by the famous chef, Julia Child.

   _____

4. The Siberian tiger quickly leapt high into the air and landed on top of the seal.

   _____

5. The new jeep was washed thoroughly by Sheila.

   _____

6. As a fitting end to the year, David Swain was dunked by his students at the school fair.

   _____

7. Iris closed her eyes as she ran her delicate fingers through the cool, clear water.

   _____

8. The Great Pyramid was built by the Egyptians.

   _____

9. The banana bread was already made by Carla before I got home.

   _____

10. Jason's letter of resignation was written hastily.

    _____

Copyright © American Book Company

WRITING INTRODUCTIONS

In Chapter 1, you learned that the beginning and the end of a paragraph are important. The same is true of an essay, where the **introduction** and the **conclusion** should each consist of one paragraph. In this section, you will learn **how to write an introduction** and about **different types of introductions**. In the next section, you will learn to write **conclusions**.

How to Write an Introduction

The **introduction** is the first paragraph of your essay. Usually, it is shorter than the body paragraphs, but it serves an important purpose. It tells the reader where you are going and invites him or her to join you. It should catch the reader's interest and clearly describe the controlling idea of the essay. The introduction may also inform the reader of the order of support for the controlling idea.

You probably have seen stores that try to attract customers by placing a huge, flourescent-colored sign outside, advertising an incredible sale. This catches the interest of potential buyers and leads them into the store. Then, the sales people can show the customers other merchandise that is of higher quality, but is also higher priced. This is what the store managers really want to sell.

This approach to sales is somewhat similar to how you want to lead a reader into your essay. You want to catch the reader's attention, lead him or her into your essay, and then, explain the purpose of your essay. A simple way to build an introduction is by using the following three components: **lead**, **tie-in**, and **controlling idea**.

Lead

Sometimes you can start your essay by stating the controlling idea of your essay, but often, that type of beginning is too abrupt. You need to grab the reader's attention first, and make the reader want to read further. You can do this with the first sentence, called a **lead**. The lead may be one of the following:

- **statement of your position on the topic**
- **problem or riddle**
- **surprising statistic or fact**
- **question**
- **brief story**
- **quotation**
- **catchy remark**
- **general, thought-provoking statement**

Tie-In

Once you have captured the reader's attention with your lead, you need to draw his or her attention to the controlling idea of your essay. You need to consider the audience, the topic of your essay, and your personal preference in developing a creative link between the lead and the statement of your controlling idea.

Controlling Idea

You practiced developing controlling ideas in the last chapter. The first paragraph is a good place to state the controlling idea because it lets the reader know the topic of the essay, your position on the topic, and how you are going to order your supporting points.

Copyright © American Book Company

Different Types of Introductions

Below you will find examples of introductions that use different types of leads followed by a tie-in and a statement of the controlling idea. The first example is labeled for you. For the other examples, circle the lead, bracket the tie-in, and underline the statement of the controlling idea.

State Your Position on the Topic

Don't let the Metropolitan Mosquito Control District spray your land! — **Lead**

They say they are protecting our children by killing mosquitoes that carry La Crosse encephalitis. Concerned citizens must ask, however, if the benefits outweigh the risks. — **Tie-in**

Despite the tremendous cost of the spraying, there has not been a significant decrease in the number of cases of encephalitis. Also, the District uses chemical pesticides that hurt our children by polluting the environment. — **Controlling Idea**

Here, the writer's position is stated directly and emphatically in the first line. This direct challenge to the reader to take action is an attention-getter. The author briefly comments on a possible objection to the argument and then states the controlling idea in the last two sentences of this brief introduction.

Problem or Riddle

Dentists recommend brushing your teeth with it. House cleaners use it to scour counter tops. You can add it to your laundry detergent to freshen your clothes. And, of course, it is an essential ingredient for many baking recipes. Sodium bicarbonate, popularly known as baking soda, is the most useful item in your household. It is especially helpful for cleaning, eliminating odors, and personal hygiene.

Unlike the introduction that states your purpose right off, the "riddle" introduction holds back one piece of information while teasing the reader to guess what it might be. Notice how this introduction gives examples that support the controlling idea, even before stating that idea in the final sentence. More examples are needed for the body paragraphs, but these are good starting places.

Surprising Statistic or Fact

In one year, firearms killed 0 children in Japan, 19 in Great Britain, 57 in Germany, 109 in France, 153 in Canada and 5,285 in the United States. In the land of the free and the home of the brave, we cling to our "right to bear arms." However, the frightening numbers that result should make us reconsider the effects of this "right." In order to protect our children, and the others who die from handguns, the United States should pass sensible gun laws that include licensing of handgun owners, registration of handguns, and limiting gun purchases to no more than one a month.

A statistic or fact is only surprising if it contradicts common beliefs or perceptions. Regarding gun violence, people who read or watch the news know that people using firearms often tragically kill children. What they may not know is that the United States is unique in this area among its primary political allies. This statistic will catch a reader's attention and make him or her want to continue reading.

Copyright © American Book Company

Question

> *Where is the safest place for a mother to give birth to a baby? You may think in a hospital, but statistics are showing that the mother's own home is just as safe, if not safer, when a trained midwife attends the birth. This may seem like a strange idea, but for tens of thousands of years, women gave birth at home. Only in the 20th century have women routinely traveled to hospitals to give birth. Now, age-old wisdom and modern science are coming together to show that for a woman who is experiencing a healthy pregnancy, her own home is the safest place to give birth because she is comfortable in a familiar environment, surrounded by people who love and support her, and free from standardized hospital policies.*

Beginning an essay with a question automatically engages the reader and makes him or her start thinking. It also creates curiosity about how you will answer the question, making the reader wonder if you will agree or disagree. In the example above, notice that the answer the author gives is a surprising fact.

Brief Story

> *When I walked into the Fairlawn nursing home for the first time, I had an uneasy feeling in my stomach. I didn't know what to expect when I entered the circular Activities Room. I found a dozen elderly people, each staring out the floor-to-ceiling picture windows that framed a variety of unique bird feeders. The Activities Director had assured me that my visit would be a great help, but I didn't know what to do. I walked over to one of the windows and spotted a small, dark gray bird with white underparts and black on top of its head. I whispered to myself, "I wonder what kind that is?" Next to me, a gray-haired, frail-looking woman smiled and said in her gravelly voice, "That's a nuthatch, my dear." Our conversation continued from there and continues each Tuesday when I visit Mrs. Joblanski. My several months of regular visits have shown me that visiting nursing homes is a great opportunity for community service because the residents love to see visitors, the staff is happy to have some help, and those who visit can learn a great deal from listening to the wisdom of older people.*

The key to beginning an essay with a brief story is to keep it *brief*. The story is not the focus of the essay, it is only a lead-in to your topic. You can increase the effectiveness of this type of introduction by including details in the story that relate to the controlling idea. Notice in the story above that the author describes examples of a resident who loves to see visitors, a welcoming staff person, and the wisdom of an older person. These details not only help introduce the controlling idea but also help to support it.

Quotation

*"You can't have dessert until you finish your vegetables,"
mothers across the nation used to say. With that kind of introduction,
no wonder so many people neglect this wonderful food group. But
they are missing so much. Fresh vegetables are packed with nutrition,
they taste good, and their production conserves natural resources.
For these reasons, fresh vegetables should be a significant part of each
person's diet.*

The quotation above is not from a famous person, but it is well-known. Any interesting
quote that you can easily relate to your topic will make a good lead for your introduction.

Catchy Phrase

*For some students, taking a standardized test is like fighting in a world war, but
as Franklin D. Roosevelt said, "We have nothing to fear but fear itself." With these
words, the President encouraged the people of the United States to victory in the
Second World War. He believed the American people had the resources and talent to
defeat Germany and Japan, if they did not let fear stop them. In a similar way,
students must overcome "test anxiety" in order to succeed. Through adequate
preparation, good health practices, and simple relaxation techniques, students can
improve their performance on standardized tests.*

This introduction uses a catchy phrase followed by a quotation. The striking contrast between
taking a test and fighting a world war sparks interest, and the quote from Roosevelt continues the
metaphor. The writer may choose to use allusions to fighting in a war later in the essay to help
connect the ideas.

General Thought-Provoking Statement

*Almost 40 years since Martin Luther King's "I Have a Dream"
speech and nearly 140 years after Abraham Lincoln's Emancipation
Proclamation, the scourge of racism still undermines the great
principles of this nation. It has become obvious that legislation
cannot erase the fear that prevents people from seeing their common
humanity. The work of changing hearts must begin at home.
Parents can teach young children tolerance and understanding by
questioning media images of race relations, purchasing multi-
cultural toys, and encouraging cross-racial friendships.*

Large issues attract large audiences. By stating a general principle, idea, or situation at the
beginning of the essay, you allow readers to connect with a familiar idea. Then, you can direct
them to the specific issue or approach you want to discuss in your essay.

> *Build your introduction with a lead, tie-in, and statement of the
> controlling idea.*

Copyright © American Book Company

PRACTICE 8: WRITING INTRODUCTIONS

For four of the topics listed below, use brainstorming or freewriting to develop a controlling idea and three supporting points. Then, write an introduction for an essay on each topic. Use a different type of lead for each introduction. (Save your work for other Practices in this chapter.)

1. Global warming: is the theory fact or fiction?

2. Use of steroids by professional athletes: does it matter and why or why not?

3. Television in schools: is it educational or political?

4. Animal rights movement: is it on target or beyond the mark?

5. Harry Potter books: innocent kids' literature or corrupting force?

6. Year-long schools: will they work or will they be another failed educational plan?

7. Dreams: are they just a passing vision or an important glimpse into the inner self?

8. The energy crisis: is it a mandate to drill for oil in national parks, or is it an opportunity to use alternate energy sources?

WRITING CONCLUSIONS

The ending of an essay is just as important as the beginning. You don't want to end your essay by running out of ideas. You want to bring your essay to a logical **conclusion**. You can imagine  your essay is like taking someone for a ride in a taxi. When you get to your destination, you don't want to slam on the brakes and tell your passenger, "Get out!" You want to announce that you are nearing the destination, ease on the brakes, and say "Good-bye" when he or she steps out of the car. This increases your chances of a good tip.

The concluding paragraph should be similar. You want to let the reader know that he or she has reached the end of the essay. Then, remind the reader about the points you have discussed along the way, but don't restate the controlling idea. Finally, leave the reader with something to do or a thought to ponder. In writing the conclusion, you can use many of the same strategies as you do for writing the introduction, but instead of saying "hello," you are saying "good-bye."

An effective way to write a concluding paragraph for a persuasive essay is to

(1) acknowledge the opposition, even mentioning a point of agreement with the opposition,
(2) comment on the reasons why your approach is better, and
(3) leave the reader with a specific action to do or a thought to ponder.

See how the authors use this pattern in the following examples. Students wrote these conclusions to end three of the essays introduced in the last section.

Copyright © American Book Company

Summarize, But Don't Restate, Your Controlling Idea

For women who are experiencing medical problems in the birth process, hospitals provide the necessary interventions to save lives. However, these interventions are unnecessary for a normal, healthy birth. In this case, a woman can have a wonderful birth experience when loved ones nurture her in her own home and a knowledgeable midwife attends to her needs.

In this example, the author admits that hospitals are important but not always necessary. The author concludes by summarizing the controlling idea. In this way, the reader leaves the essay with the controlling idea being his or her last thought, making it more easily remembered.

Give the Audience a Question to Ponder

Citizens of the United States fiercely protect their right to individual freedom. Independent-minded people formed this country by telling Great Britain to leave them alone and stop interfering in their lives. This rich tradition of liberty should be protected, but not at the expense of our children. Sensible gun laws place reasonable limitations on the purchase of fire arms. These laws do not abolish the "right to bear arms;" they simply protect our children. How many more children must die before the government steps in to protect them?

The author of this conclusion agrees that personal liberty is important, but the law should place reasonable limitations on it. The author leaves the reader with a heart-wrenching question to ponder.

Urge the Audience to Take Action

The idea of spraying a few mosquitoes to protect children from a terrible disease seems like a good idea at first. However, when you consider the small number of cases of encephalitis, the cost to the taxpayer, and the damage to the environment, spraying does not appear to be the best answer. The District will continue its work unless we make our voices heard. Call the District today to tell them not to spray your land.

Often in a persuasive essay, your intent is not just to convince the audience to agree with your position but also to encourage the audience to take action. After you have argued your position, you can urge the reader to take the action you want him or her to take.

In your conclusion, acknowledge the opposition, comment on the reasons why your approach is better, and leave the reader with a specific action to do or a thought to ponder.

Copyright © American Book Company

PRACTICE 9: WRITING CONCLUSIONS

Using your ideas from Practice 8 on page 87, write conclusions to match the introductions you wrote. Experiment with different types of conclusions. (Save your work for Practice 13.)

USING TRANSITIONAL WORDS

In Chapter 3, you saw how an outline is like a road map guiding you as you write your essay. As you write your draft, remember that your reader does not have a road map. It is not enough for you just to write a series of ideas. You need to lead the reader through your essay by showing how the ideas are related to each other. **Transitional words** help the reader see the relationship between your ideas. These relationships include **time order, order of importance, cause and effect, comparison,** and **contrast.**

Time Order

You can use transitional words to show **time order**, that is when events happen in relation to each other: one event before another, one after another, or both at the same time. Read the following example to see what happens when transitional words are missing.

Example 1:   *Our family has a daily routine to get us to work and school. My father leaves the house. He wakes up my brother and me. I get up and take a shower. My brother takes a shower. I get dressed. My mother gets our lunches ready. We eat breakfast. We jump in the car and drive to school. Mom drops us off on her way to work.*

Example 1 is choppy because it is missing transitional words to clarify the order of events. Without these words, the reader wonders how the father can leave the house and then wake up his sons. Below is a corrected example with transitional words underlined.

Example 2:   *Our family has a daily routine to get us to work and school. <u>Before</u> my father leaves the house, he wakes up my brother and me. I get up <u>first</u> and take a shower. <u>Then</u>, my brother takes a shower <u>while</u> I'm getting dressed. <u>Meanwhile</u>, my mother gets our lunches ready. <u>After</u> breakfast, we jump in the car and drive to school. <u>Finally</u>, Mom drops us off on her way to work.*

Using transitional words is a simple and effective way to present your ideas and descriptions clearly. The chart below provides you with examples of transitional words that show time order.

Transitional Words for Time Order			
after	again	and then	as
as long as	as soon as	at the same time	before
currently	during	eventually	finally
first	gradually	immediately	in the future
later	meanwhile	now	second
soon	suddenly	then	third
until	when	whenever	while

Copyright © American Book Company

Order of Importance

In Chapter 1, you saw how to structure ideas in a paragraph according to their **order of importance**. Transitional words help show which idea you want to emphasize as more important than others. The example below lacks these transitional words.

Example 3:   *You should always be aware of your surroundings in parking lots at night. Look over the lot carefully for potential danger spots, such as areas of low visibility and areas which do not have parking attendants. Be sure you have a defensive weapon, such as pepper spray or a loud noisemaker, in your hand as you walk to your vehicle. Before entering your vehicle, look through the windows to make sure no one is hiding inside.*

Notice how in Example 3 the writer did not use transitional words to indicate whether one of the steps is more important than another. Below is a corrected example with underlined transitional words showing the order of importance.

Example 4:   *You should always be aware of your surroundings in parking lots at night. <u>First</u>, look over the lot carefully for potential danger spots, such as areas of low visibility and areas which do not have parking attendants. <u>More importantly</u>, be sure you have a defensive weapon, such as pepper spray or a loud noisemaker, in your hand as you walk to your vehicle. <u>Above all</u>, before entering your vehicle, look through the windows to make sure no one is hiding inside.*

As you can see, using these transitional words helps to rank the steps required to reduce the potential danger of parking lots at night.

Transitional Words for Order of Importance

above all	especially	first
in fact	in particular	of highest importance
more importantly	most importantly	

Cause and Effect

Linking **causes and effects** is an important aspect of writing a convincing persuasive essay. You can use transitional words to make these connections clear. Read the example below.

Example 5:   *Local graffiti "artists" are becoming more brazen. Two weeks ago, they sprayed paint across three community centers. Last week, several businesses found their buildings "decorated" against their wishes. Last night, some graffiti writers took their work inside, painting the twelfth floor of the Twin Tower building. The city council announced a special hearing for Thursday of next week to discuss possible responses to this problem.*

Copyright © American Book Company

The cause and effect relationship in Example 5 is not clear because the paragraph is missing a crucial transition. Read Example 6, and notice how just one transitional phrase (underlined) can bring clarity to this paragraph by signaling the effect of the graffiti writers' activities.

Example 6:   *Local graffiti "artists" are becoming more brazen. Two weeks ago, they sprayed paint across three community centers. Last week, several businesses found their buildings "decorated" against their wishes. Last night, some graffiti writers took their work inside to the twelfth floor of the Twin Tower building. As a result, the city council announced a special hearing for Thursday of next week to discuss possible responses to this problem.*

Because the writer added one transitional phrase in Example 6, the whole paragraph is clearer. The phrase "as a result" shows that the city council's announcement is an effect of the graffiti writing.

Transitional Words for Cause and Effect				
as a result	because	for this reason	if, then	since
so	so that	therefore	thus	whenever

Comparison

Transitional words help a writer show **comparisons,** or differences, of how certain ideas or subjects are similar. Example 7 lacks these transitions.

Example 7:   *The United States and the USSR did not want to enter World War II. They had been forced to enter the fighting because of sneak attacks. The Soviets were caught off guard when Hitler broke his non-aggression treaty and invaded the Soviet Union on June 22, 1941. The United States suffered a surprise attack when the Japanese struck the US naval base at Pearl Harbor on December 7, 1941. From that time on, the two countries were allies in fighting the Axis powers of Germany, Italy, and Japan.*

Due to the lack of transitional words in Example 7, the similarities between the United States' and the Soviet Union's entry into World War II are not as clear as they could be. In fact, the first sentence is awkward. The few well-placed transitions shown in Example 8 make the passage much more effective and easily understood.

Example 8:   *Neither the United States nor the USSR had wanted to enter World War II. Both countries had been forced to enter the fighting because of sneak attacks. The Soviets were caught off guard when Hitler broke his non-aggression treaty and invaded the Soviet Union on June 22, 1941. Similarly, the United States suffered a surprise attack when the Japanese struck the US naval base at Pearl Harbor on December 7, 1941. From that time on, the two countries were allies in fighting the Axis powers of Germany, Italy, and Japan.*

"Neither" and "nor" may not sound like comparison words, but they point to negative similarity. The other underlined transitional words make the comparisons between the US and the USSR clearer. Also, note the importance of "from that time on" in the last sentence to show the order of events.

Transitional Words for Comparison		
also	as well as	at the same time
both	equally important	in the same way
likewise	neither/nor	similarly

Contrast

Transitional words also help a writer make **contrasts,** or differences, clearer. Read the example below to see how a contrasting paragraph needs transitions.

Example 9: *You may consider caves and mines the same kind of holes in the ground. They are really quite different. Underground streams and rivers form coves over millions of years through erosion. Humans using machines dig mines over the course of only a few months. The rapid removal of rock during the mining process requires the use of supports to prevent a mine's ceiling from collapsing. The slow, natural formation of caves makes these supports unnecessary. The slow process of cave formation allows natural gases to escape slowly and safely. Miners must be cautious of the explosive and poisonous gases that are rapidly released as the earth is blasted open. As you can see, human development of the earth is often rapid and dangerous. Nature's development can be gradual and peaceful.*

Example 9 makes sense without transitional words, but it does not flow well. The writer lists the ideas, but they are not connected. Read Example 10 to see how transitional words can help the flow of the ideas in the paragraph.

Example 10: *You may consider caves and mines the same kind of holes in the ground, <u>but in reality</u>, they are quite different. Underground streams and rivers form caves over millions of years through erosion. <u>In contrast</u>, humans using machines dig mines over the course of only a few months. The rapid removal of rock during the mining process requires the use of supports to prevent a mine's ceiling from collapsing. <u>However</u>, the slow, natural formation of caves makes these supports unnecessary. The slow process of cave formation <u>also</u> allows natural gases to escape slowly and safely, <u>whereas</u> miners must be cautious of the explosive and poisonous gases that are rapidly released as the earth is blasted open. As you can see, human development of the earth is often rapid and dangerous, <u>while</u> nature's development can be gradual and peaceful.*

Copyright © American Book Company

Transitional Words for Contrast

although	and yet	but	despite
even so	even	though	however
in contrast	instead of	in spite of	nevertheless
on the one hand	on the other hand	rather than	still
whereas	while		

Use transitional words to help the reader see the relationship between your ideas. These relationships include time order, order of importance, cause and effect, comparison, and contrast.

PRACTICE 10: TRANSITIONAL WORDS

Read the paragraphs below. Decide how each paragraph would be best organized, whether by *time order, order of importance, cause and effect, comparison,* or *contrast*. Then, rewrite the paragraph on a separate sheet of paper, inserting the correct transitional words or phrases.

1.   There are many things to remember as you get ready to go back to school. Develop a positive attitude about the upcoming school year. Make sure you understand your class schedule. You know your classes. You should buy plenty of school supplies such as pens, paper, notebooks, and a calculator. Take time to inventory your clothes, and make sure you have the clothes you need. These tasks are completed. You will be ready for the new school year.

2.   Both your beliefs and your actions are important in leading an exemplary life. Your beliefs should guide you to knowing how to act in all situations. If your actions do not match what you believe, people will not listen to what you say. If you act in a way that seems good to others, but you have no beliefs to explain your actions, people may label you as shallow. Be certain and careful with both your beliefs and your actions in order to be an example to others.

3.   Watching television at my grandmother's house was always a family event. Her TV was so old it didn't even have remote control! My family fought over what show to watch. We were used to watching two or three channels at the same time, while using the remote control. Grandma didn't have cable. We had to twist and turn the antenna and our bodies, just to get a decent picture. Two of us were on the sofa watching TV and somebody else sat in the recliner. The TV screen would get all fuzzy. We all had to pile onto the sofa. We could avoid these problems with the television and the family fights. We bought Grandma a new television (with remote control!) and a year's cable service. Our visits to Grandma's are much more peaceful, though, in a way, we miss the wrangling.

Copyright © American Book Company

4.   I like to prioritize the duties I feel towards those around me. I feel duty-bound to care for and protect my parents, brothers, and sisters. I try to take care of my extended family and close friends. I consider it necessary to serve my country in the case of foreign attack. These three circles of obligation complete the priorities I feel in my social and civic life.

5.   Ordering something as simple as a pizza requires several steps. You should look through the tower of coupons that has grown from daily advertisement mailings. You must endure the arduous process of finding out what everyone wants on their pizza. Call the pizza place and wait on hold. You are ready to hang up and make your own pizza. Distract your mind from the growing hunger in your stomach by getting your money ready. The delivery person arrives, run out to the car, grab the pizza, and shove the money in the person's hand. You can enjoy the lukewarm pizza that you earned with all your hard work.

6.   The preparation required for a test is quite similar to the preparation needed for a sports event. Training for any sports event requires daily practice to keep the athlete's body in good condition. Test preparation requires daily practice and review to keep the scholar's memory up to date. The night before a sporting event, the athlete must get plenty of rest. A scholar must rest his or her mind, so it will be fresh for the big event of the test. A good athlete will take pride in a nutritious diet that provides the building blocks for a strong body. A scholar must feed the mind with nutritious food to increase mental skill. Test-taking may not have the same glamour as athletic competition, but both activities require preparation in order to achieve success.

PRACTICE 11: TRANSITIONAL WORDS

A.   On your own, or in small groups, skim through articles in newspapers, in magazines, or on the Internet. Find paragraphs that contain transitional words based on each of the following: *time order*, *order of importance*, *comparison and contrast*, or *cause and effect*. Share these paragraphs with your teacher or other students. Do the transitional words improve your understanding of the paragraph? Why or why not?

B.   On your own, or in small groups, write four different paragraphs. Each paragraph should include transitional words from the different categories discussed in this chapter: *time order*, *order of importance*, *comparison and contrast*, or *cause and effect*. Return to the lists of these words to help you. Then, exchange your collection of paragraphs with your teacher or with another group, and grade the paragraphs by evaluating how well the transitional words are used within each paragraph.

Here are some possible topics for each of your four paragraphs:

Time Order
Your first driving lesson
A time you got lost

Order of Importance
Prioritize your duties for today
Who are the three most important people in your life? Why?

Comparison and Contrast
Do you prefer pizza or hamburgers? Why?
Which is better on a Friday night–watching television at home or going out to a movie?

Cause and Effect
Why is a high school diploma important?
What are the effects of sports programs on high school students?

Copyright © American Book Company

DEVELOPING COHERENCE

Coherence means to stick together. You want the ideas of your essay to "stick together," that is, to be connected and to lead from one to the other. Tying your ideas together is an important part of helping the reader understand your writing. Three ways you can link the ideas and paragraphs in your essay are **planning an order**, **using transitions**, and **repeating key words and phrases**.

Planning an Order

In Chapter 1, you practiced four different ways to organize ideas: spatial order, time order, order of importance, or contrasting ideas. Organizing your ideas in a certain order is the first step to developing a coherent essay.

Using Transitions

In the last section, you saw how transitional words link ideas from one sentence to another. They also link ideas between paragraphs to make the whole essay "stick together." Without these transitional words and phrases, the writing becomes less interesting or even less understandable.

Repeating Key Words or Phrases

While you don't want to say the same thing over and over, repeating certain key words and phrases can improve the reader's understanding of the topic. By including key words or ideas from your controlling idea in the topic sentences of your paragraphs, you will make it easier for the reader to follow your train of thought. These repeated words are like landmarks along the road of your essay, reminding the reader where you have been and where you are going. For example, look at the following plan for an essay in which the topic sentences repeat key words from the controlling idea:

Controlling Idea: *Citizens of the United States could greatly improve the country by obeying the law, protecting the environment, and being kind to other people.*

Topic Sentence: *The first and most basic step to improving the country is to obey the law.*

Topic Sentence: *In addition to obeying the law, citizens can make this country even more beautiful by protecting the environment.*

Topic Sentence: *A third way to make the United States a better place to live is for citizens to reach beyond their own self-interest and be kind to one another.*

You can also repeat key words or phrases throughout the essay, not only in the topic sentences.

> *Develop coherence (link the ideas and paragraphs) in your essay by planning an order, using transitional words, and repeating key words and phrases.*

PRACTICE 12: DEVELOPING COHERENCE

Read the following essay. Decide how the writer ordered ideas in the essay. Then, (circle) transitional words, and underline repeated words.

Where is the safest place for a mother to give birth to her baby? You may think in a hospital, but the facts show that the mother's own home is just as safe, if not safer, when a trained midwife attends the birth. This may seem like a strange idea, but for tens of thousands of years, women gave birth at home. Only in recent centuries have women traveled to hospitals to give birth. Age old wisdom and modern science are coming together to show that for a woman who is experiencing a healthy pregnancy, her own home is the safest place to give birth because she is comfortable in a familiar environment, surrounded by people who love and support her, and free from standardized hospital policies.

Women who are in the midst of labor must feel safe and comfortable, or they will have interrupted labor. This fact is recognized in the animal world but often neglected in regard to human mothers. For example, when a doe feels labor coming on, she seeks out a secure and protected place to give birth to her offspring. If she detects a predator approaching, her contractions will stop, so that she can run away and find another safe spot. Once she is settled in, her labor will resume. In a similar way, many women progress well in their labor at home, but when they arrive at the hospital their labor slows down. Sometimes, the hospital even sends the woman back home, where her contractions again progress normally. The disruption and anxiety of the trip to the hospital can cause a woman's labor to slow or halt. If she can remain in the safety and comfort of her home throughout labor and delivery, her birth experience will probably follow a more natural and rhythmic pattern.

A more important factor in the woman's feeling of safety and comfort is the presence of loving and supportive friends and family. This may seem like a nice extra that has little biological effect on the birthing process, but there are significant differences between births of women with and without help. The comforting presence of a friend or family member leads to less need for anesthetic drugs and fewer surgical deliveries, called cesarean sections. Many hospitals still place limitations on who can be with the mother while she is giving birth. There is also little space in one hospital room. At home, friends and family are welcome to come and go as the mother chooses, not as the hospital chooses.

The number of people allowed to be with the mother is just one restriction hospital policies place on birthing mothers. Freedom from these restrictive policies is probably the best part of giving birth at home. Hospitals require birthing mothers to eat nothing more than ice chips during labor, so that the mother's stomach is empty in case she needs general anesthesia for an emergency cesarean section. This lack of food causes the mother to lose the energy she needs to deliver the baby, which, in turn, increases the need for a cesarean section. Furthermore, hospitals require women to lie down in bed for electronic monitoring of the baby. The electronic monitoring allows fewer nurses to be on staff and provides insurance companies with a record of the baby's health. However, it prevents the mother from walking–a natural way of using motion and gravity to ease the birthing process. Finally, hospitals routinely use drugs which greatly affect the tiny baby and cause the mother to be less able to push. These policies can benefit some women, but when they are applied to all women across the board, they can make labor more difficult. Under the care of a midwife at home, a woman has more flexibility with procedures that will aid her unique birth.

For women who are experiencing medical problems in the birth process, hospitals provide the necessary interventions to save lives. However, these interventions are unnecessary for a normal, healthy birth. In this case, a woman can have a wonderful birth experience with loved ones nurturing her in her own home and with a knowledgeable midwife attending to her needs.

Copyright © American Book Company

WRITING THE DRAFT

After practicing the many different aspects of drafting, you are ready to write your own draft. Remember, when you write a draft, it does not have to be perfect on the first try. You have time to revise and proofread later. Focus on getting your ideas onto paper. As you write, leave wide margins, as well as space between each line, so you have room to make changes later. As you practice writing, you can develop your own personal writing process. Some writers follow their clustering directly. Other writers begin writing the body paragraphs, write a strong conclusion, and then go back and write an introduction. There are no rules for this part of writing. Find the best way for you to get your ideas on paper.

Before you get started, let's return to the essay topic about the effects of television on young viewers. As you will recall, the controlling idea was stated as follows:

Television affects young children negatively by exposing them to adult programs, increasing their desire for needless products, and decreasing their playful activity.

Based on this controlling idea and the outline that appeared in Chapter 3, a student wrote the following draft.

Television affects young children negatively by exposing them to adult programs, increasing their desire for needless products, and decreasing their playful activity. Little kids watch a lot of television. Television can be great for teaching kids numbers and letters and sometimes even manners. Kids learn other things from television, too. Besides that, they could be doing a lot of other good things other than watching television.

People get killd all the time on TV, children are watching Sesame Street or Barney or some other cartoon, and on comes a commercial for an adult show that will be on later that night. In those few seconds, children exposed to theft, murder, and sex that they shouldn't see.

Another important question to ask about TV and small children is what they are <u>not</u> doing while they are watching television. Children especially between the ages of two and five are growing very quick and need to exercise their growing muscles. They learn by doing, not by sitting. When children sit in front of a televison, they are not running or jumping. They are not exploring the world outside or learining motor skills developed through puzzles or blocks. Further, therye not learning the social skill of playing with other children. Children may watch tv together, but it does not require them to interact with each other.

Commercials are another problem with television. Commercials advertise other shows with adult content in them, commercials tell kids to buy all this stuff theat they don't need. Thats' how television pays for itself. Companies pay to put commercials on tv and they hope kids will buy their stuff. The commercials tell kids that they will be happy if they buy the stuff. They will be like other kids and they will be liked by other kids if they have this stuff. It is difficult enough for addults to tell the difference between reality and fiction in commercials. How is a three-year-old supposed to do that?

Copyright © American Book Company

Some shows on television may be educational or entertaining for children, but libraries and schools are much better places for kids to learn. Kids can learn a lot from computers, too. Although some problems with television are the same for computers. Violence, sex and commercials are important problems with television. Little kids shouldn't watch much television. They should be outside playing.

This draft has many errors that you can detect easily as you read. These errors are typical of any draft. That is why revising and proofreading are so important. In the next two chapters, you will practice these skills. For now, let your ideas flow from your outlines onto the paper as you write your drafts for Practice 13.

> **As you write a draft, leave wide margins, as well as space between each line, so that you have room to make changes later.**

PRACTICE 13: WRITING THE DRAFT

A. In Practice 8 and Practice 9, you created an introduction and a conclusion for four different essays. Return to your introductions, conclusions, and brainstorming lists, and develop outlines for two or more essays on the four topics. Then, draft the body paragraphs. Remember, your essays don't have to be perfect. However, pay attention to the skills you practiced in this chapter.

Use the following checklist as you write each essay.

☐ I used specific words.

☐ I avoided clichés and sweeping generalizations.

☐ I used active voice.

☐ I developed a clear introduction.

☐ I wrote an appropriate conclusion.

☐ I used transitional words to link ideas together.

☐ I wrote a coherent essay.

☐ I left wide margins and space between each line, so I can make corrections more easily.

B. Return to Practice 5: Making a Plan on page 70 in Chapter 3. In this exercise, you developed outlines and clustering diagrams for four different topics. Now, use these plans to draft an essay for one or more of the topics. Use the checklist above to help you.

C. For further practice and instruction in writing, visit two of the Web sites, or consult one of the books listed in Appendix B: Writing Resources (pages 185-188).

Copyright © American Book Company

CHAPTER 4 SUMMARY: DRAFTING THE ESSAY

- *Improve your word choice by using specific words, using a dictionary and thesaurus, being aware of connotations and denotations, and avoiding clichés and sweeping generalizations.*

- *Use active voice.*

- *Build your introduction with a lead, tie-in, and statement of the controlling idea.*

- *In your conclusion, acknowledge the opposition, comment on the reasons why your approach is better, and leave the reader with a specific action to do or a thought to ponder.*

- *Use transitional words to help the reader see the relationship between your ideas. These relationships include time order, order of importance, cause and effect, comparison, and contrast.*

- *Develop coherence (link the ideas and paragraphs) in your essay by planning an order, using transitional words, and repeating words and phrases.*

- *As you write a draft, leave wide margins, as well as space between each line, so that you have room to make changes later.*

CHAPTER 4 REVIEW: DRAFTING THE ESSAY

For the Chapter Review in Chapter 3: Planning the Essay, you prepared brainstorming lists, freewriting samples, clustering diagrams, outlines, and outline shortcuts for five different writing prompts. Based on these prewriting activities, write a draft of an essay for one or more of the writing prompts. Use the skills you practiced in this chapter. You may also use the checklist below which is reproduced from page 98.

- ☐   I used specific words.

- ☐   I avoided clichés and sweeping generalizations.

- ☐   I used active voice.

- ☐   I developed a clear introduction.

- ☐   I wrote an appropriate conclusion.

- ☐   I used transitional words to link ideas together.

- ☐   I wrote a coherent essay.

- ☐   I left wide margins and space between each line, so I can make corrections more easily.

Note: You will revise these drafts in the Chapter 5 Review, so keep them in a safe place, such as your portfolio.

Copyright © American Book Company

ADDITIONAL ACTIVITIES: DRAFTING THE ESSAY

1. Rewrite the following paragraph, using vivid images and concrete words to enhance the description.

    The trees line both sides of the street, giving shade to all who pass by. The trees also shade the houses in the neighborhood. Birds play in the air and make their usual noises. Woods surround the neighborhood, and in these woods there is a small pond. Sometimes children will swim there, or sail toy boats across the pond. There is usually a breeze blowing across.

2. This paragraph below contains clichés and sweeping generalizations. Rewrite the paragraph in Standard American English.

    I have a bone to pick with Lindsey Savage. Two shakes of a lamb's tail after his election, he is raising a ruckus. "The county roads need fixing," he says, "so let's add 1% to the sales tax." Lindsey Savage is so crooked he has to screw on his socks. The extra money for road improvements will just go to line the pockets of his sidekicks in the road construction business. Then they'll just piddle around and waste our money. If you hate more taxes, make a beeline for the county commission meeting next Tuesday night. Voice your opinions, or we're up the creek without a paddle.

3. On your own or in a group, skim through 3-4 articles in magazines such as *Time, Newsweek, People, Sports Illustrated*, etc. Find an article that has an effective introduction and conclusion. In 3-4 sentences, explain why they are effective. Then share your findings with your class or instructor.

4. Use the same articles from number 3, and describe how the articles develop coherence. List 3-4 examples of how the author uses transitional words and repeats certain key words or phrases. Also describe how the author ordered his or her ideas. Share your findings with the class or instructor.

Chapter 5
Revising the Essay

Even if you plan your essay very carefully and try to write your draft precisely, you will still have room for improvement. The professional readers who grade essays for the Georgia High School Writing Test will look only at your final product. You want them to see your *best* effort, not your *first* effort. Remember, writing is a process of thinking, writing, and reviewing. Once the draft is finished, it is time for reviewing which includes **revising** and **proofreading**. This chapter will help you with revising, and the next chapter will show you how to proofread.

Revising is looking again at the draft of your essay with the intention of making changes to improve it. Revising involves:

- **Adding Clarifying Information**
- **Deleting Unrelated Sentences**
- **Eliminating Unnecessary Words**
- **Correcting Shifts in Tense or Person**
- **Checking for Parallel Sentence Structure**
- **Developing Sentence Variety**

HOW TO REVISE

Before revising your draft, you may want to take a short break of a minute or so to think about something else. Then, return to your essay, and read it as if you were the audience. Put yourself in the place of the people who will be reading it, and read as if you were seeing the essay for the first time. Make your changes by using the spaces in between the lines and in the margins. While you read your essay during the revising stage, ask yourself the following questions:

1. **Is the introduction a good preview of the rest of the essay?**
2. **Does my statement of the controlling idea give my essay a clear purpose?**
3. **Do the body paragraphs support the controlling idea with logically arranged supporting details?**
4. **Will my audience clearly understand how my ideas fit together?**
5. **Is there any irrelevant or repeated information that I can cut out?**
6. **Is there information that I need to add to make my ideas clearer?**
7. **Do my sentences fall into a repetitive and uninteresting pattern?**
8. **Have I used transitional words appropriately?**
9. **How can I improve my word choice?**
10. **Are there unexpected shifts in person or tense?**
11. **Are there unnecessary words that I can delete?**
12. **Does my conclusion tie the essay together and leave the reader with an action or thought to consider?**

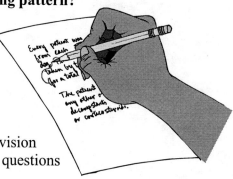

Return to the draft of the essay about how watching television affects young children on pages 97-98, and consider the questions above.

Copyright © American Book Company

As you looked over the draft, you probably noticed the following:

In the **first paragraph** of the sample essay, the controlling idea is clearly stated. However, an introduction is stronger when it begins by getting the reader's attention and leads up to a statement of the controlling idea, usually in the last sentence of the first paragraph.

The **second paragraph** begins with a broad generalization that does not provide a good connection with the first paragraph. The details which follow are a good start, but they could be improved with more description.

The **third paragraph** and **fourth paragraph both** have some significant grammar and spelling errors that need to be corrected. More significantly, the fourth paragraph, which addresses commercials, should follow the second paragraph, which also deals with commercials. Rearranging ideas, even paragraphs, is appropriate for the revising step in the writing process.

The **conclusion** strays away from the topic by introducing subjects that haven't been discussed in the essay, such as libraries and computers. The conclusion should not introduce new ideas or information but tie previously developed arguments together into a strong ending. You want to leave the reader with something he or she can remember easily.

Considering these improvements, a revised essay might look something like this:

"Hey kids, let's count to ten! One, two, three . . ." Sure television can be great for teaching children numbers and letters. Some tv shows even teach children manners. But what else do children learn from TV? Does television harm children? And what could they be doing instead of watching TV? Television affects young children negatively by exposing them to violence, sex, and commercials, and by decreasing their playful activity.

Even though children may be watching shows appropriate for their age, they still have the opportunity to see programs that are meant only for adults. A young child may be enjoying Sesame Street, but in changing the channel to watch Barney, he or she sees commercials for adult shows that will be on later that night. Two teens run up to car, throw the driver out, jump in themselves and drive away. Next, mean looking faces shout angry words, guns flash and person lies dead. Finally, a man and a woman being taking off each other's clothes. In these few seconds, the children is exposed to theft, murder, and sex that children shouldn't see.

Commercicals are another problem with television. As well as advertising shows with adult content, commercials persuade children to buy products theat they do not need. Thats' how television pays for itself. Companies pay to put commercials on television and they hope children will buy there stuff. The voice on commercials tell children that they will be happy if they buy a certain toy or cereal. They will be like other children. And other children will like them if they have those products. It is difficult enough for adults to tell the difference between reality fiction in commercials. How are a three-year-old supposed to do that?

Copyright © American Book Company

Another important question to ask about TV and small children is what they are not doing while they are watching television. Children especially between the ages of two and five are growing very quickly and need to exercise their growing muscles. They learn by doing, not by sitting. When children sit in front of a television, they are not running or jumping. They are not exploring the world outside or lerning motor skills developed through puzzles or blocks. Further, therye not learning the social skill of playing with other children. Children may watch television together, but it does not require them to enteract with each other.

Some shows on television may be educational or entertaining for children. Hoowever, inbetween these shows their commercials with adult content and violent images. In addition, other commericals teach children the false idea that byying all kinds of products will make them happy. And even if children could only watch educational shows without commercials, they would learn more and be more heathy if they went outside to play with their freinds.

There are still some errors in the essay which the next chapter will address. For the rest of this chapter, you will practice some revising skills.

ADDING CLARIFYING INFORMATION

When you write your draft, *you* know what you mean, but you want to be sure it will be clear to your audience. As you revise your essay, imagine that you are the intended audience reading the essay for the first time. You want to make sure the reader has enough information, so that she or he has no unanswered questions. Ask yourself if added information, more details, or another example would make your writing clearer. The following sentence provides a good example.

Example 1:   *At its next meeting, the school board will consider the proposal.*

The writer may have provided enough information for someone who is familiar with the situation described. However, another reader might ask, *"Which school board?" "What proposal?"* or *"When's the next meeting?"* The writer must add information to make the description clearer, as in the following sentence.

Example 2:   *Next Thursday night, the city school board will consider the proposal to expand the recycling program in all schools.*

With this sentence, the reader doesn't have to be a member of that particular school district in order to understand what the writer is describing. All the necessary information is provided. You want to write the same kind of sentences for the reader of your essay.

> **Make sure you provide the audience with enough information to understand your ideas.**

Copyright © American Book Company

PRACTICE 1: ADDING CLARIFYING INFORMATION

Revise the following sentences by adding clarifying information.

1. I went with Rafael and Scott to our favorite hang out, and we saw Priscilla.

   _____

   _____

2. The plants withered because of the drought.

   _____

   _____

3. Few people have big families these days.

   _____

   _____

4. Trees clean the air.

   _____

   _____

5. I bought a new lens to take better pictures.

   _____

   _____

DELETING UNRELATED SENTENCES

In some cases, you may want to add information, ideas, or examples to your sentences. In other cases, you will want to eliminate information, ideas, or examples if they do not relate directly to the topic of your essay. Look at the paragraph below.

> *I got a lot of great deals at the Clothing Mart. All the shoes were 50% off, so I bought two new pairs. I bought 4 new shirts because they were on sale–buy one, get one free. I'm so glad my friend, Chris, was there to help me pick out clothes. The pants were reduced by only 10%, but I really liked a green pair, so I bought it. I've never seen such a great sale.*

Each sentence in the paragraph relates to the writer's purchasing new clothes at a big sale. The author's appreciation of Chris' help, however, does not fit well in the paragraph. This sentence is not related closely enough to the other sentences, so it weakens the coherence of the paragraph. Deleting the fourth sentence will make the paragraph more concise and coherent.

> ***Delete sentences or phrases that are not directly related to the paragraph or essay.***

Copyright © American Book Company

PRACTICE 2: DELETING UNRELATED SENTENCES

Read each of the following paragraphs, and draw a line through the unrelated sentence.

1.   Out of all the classes you take in high school, not <u>one</u> of them deals with real-life situations. For example, you can get your diploma and not once have you been taught how to apply for college admission or for a full-time job. It seems like no one knows what's going on! Also, nobody has taught you how to communicate effectively or what skills are necessary in the interview process. Even if you get a job or go to college, no one has taught you how to get a checking account, apply for a lease, or even file your federal and state tax returns. It's a wonder any of us can make it to adulthood given our lack of education!

2.   My first day in high school was pretty challenging. For the first time, I changed to a different class every fifty minutes. The school was huge, and I got lost during every move. I showed up to every class late. To top it all off, the combination to my locker didn't work, so I had to carry all of my books the entire day. I was not looking forward to going home, either, because I had to mow the lawn. My only consolation was that the other students in my classes were really friendly, and the teachers were understanding of what happens that first day.

3.   When Leah turned the corner and entered the perfume shop at the mall, she got more than she bargained for. The most horrid smell in the world assaulted her nose. Customers and sales associates in this store were coughing and gagging! Leah pinched her nose immediately and ran for her life. After running for about fifty feet with her nose pinched, she released her nose and breathed some fresh air. There's nothing like fresh air to increase your mental functioning. After that incident, Leah thought it would be best to go home. Then, the next morning, she read about someone placing a stink bomb in the store as a prank.

4.   I look forward to a solution to the problem of the super-sensitive security motion sensor. Once that type of motion sensor is activated, the slightest movement can set it off. A flying moth or even my cat scratching the litter box after a large dinner can send loud sounds pulsating through my house. I know the sensor needs to detect the sounds and motions of a thief, but how many thieves are actually as small as a moth or as silent as a cat? A home security system is very expensive.

5.   Tuan liked to check his tires before driving across Seattle's harbor. When Tuan stepped out of the car, he saw something that really surprised him. He had stopped on the bridge and had a great view of Seattle's marine life. He saw an entire family of dolphins and sea otters swimming and catching fish right below him. The coastal breeze brushed Tuan's hair and sent the bridge swaying slightly under his feet. Sea gulls swooped down to participate in the feeding frenzy under the bridge. The sun's rays glistened brightly on the blue water below. Tuan captured many memorable photographs of this beautiful scene.

Copyright © American Book Company

ELIMINATING UNNECESSARY WORDS

Along with unrelated sentences, you want to eliminate unnecessary words. Good writing does not necessarily involve lengthy sentences full of big words. Good writing expresses ideas clearly through effective words–the fewer the better. As an example, read the following sentence.

Example 1: *As I was reflecting the other day, I thought about the very great number of people who, as of yet, have had very little experience of their own with using the Internet by going on-line.*

This sentence includes various words that do not help the reader understand the writer's intended idea. In fact, these extra words cloud the meaning. Read the following sentence without the extra words.

Example 2: *Two days ago, I thought about the many people who have never used the Internet.*

This shorter sentence provides the same information, but it does so more directly and clearly.

As you write your rough draft, don't worry too much about extra words. Let the ideas flow. However, when you are revising, eliminate unnecessary words, and replace them with a simpler way of expressing the same ideas. Use the chart below to help you.

Unnecessary Words	Simple Language
due to the fact that	because
with respect to	about
hurried quickly	hurried
at that point in time	then
conduct an investigation	investigate
circular in shape	circular
there are many students who join	many students join
has a preference for	prefers
it is my belief that	I believe that
she is the kind of person who doesn't tolerate rudeness	she doesn't tolerate rudeness
In Nathaniel Hawthorne's novel *The Scarlet Letter*, he writes about	In *The Scarlet Letter*, Nathaniel Hawthorne writes about

Good writing expresses ideas clearly through effective words–the fewer the better.

PRACTICE 3: ELIMINATING UNNECESSARY WORDS

Rewrite the following sentences, and eliminate the unnecessary words.

1. I received various and many compliments while attending the cast party due to the fact that the peers of my own age have a preference for acting that is less formal in style.

    _____

    _____

2. At this point in time, the county commissioners are taking into consideration the reasons for or against pursuing formal and official charges against the sheriff.

    _____

    _____

3. These are the issues that will determine who will be elected President.

    _____

    _____

4. In my mind, I was thinking that the class's poor results on the tests that were administered in physics class were due in large part to the short amount of preparation time.

    _____

    _____

5. There are many people who have homes in the urban downtown area due to the fact that they can live in close proximity to work.

    _____

    _____

Copyright © American Book Company

CORRECTING SHIFTS IN TENSE OR PERSON

Remember the image of giving the reader a taxi cab ride through your essay on page 87)? While you are "driving," you don't want to shift gears abruptly. You want to keep the ride smooth, not giving the reader any unexpected surprises. One way to do this is to avoid shifts in **tense** or **person**.

Shifts in Tense

It is important to keep **one verb tense** throughout your essay. Once you choose present or past tense, stay with it. Read the following passage, and notice how the underlined verbs shift from present tense to past tense.

Example 1: *It <u>is</u> the last game of the championship. Tamara, the girl who <u>is</u> always picked last when forming teams, <u>sits</u> on the bench and <u>cheers</u> her team, the Rockets, against the visiting team, the Panthers. Earlier in the game, Louise, the star pitcher of the Rockets, <u>sprained</u> her arm in the opening pitch. Now, in the last inning with a one run Rockets advantage and bases loaded, her replacement, Jenny, also <u>sprained</u> her arm. In a desperate move, Dalia, the coach of the Rockets, <u>told</u> Tamara, "Try your best honey. Just try not to break your hand when you throw the ball."*

The shifts in tense make the reader unsure about how the narrator is related to the action. See how much more smoothly the passage below reads because it keeps the same tense.

Example 2: *It <u>was</u> the last game of the championship. Tamara, the girl who <u>was</u> always picked last when forming teams, <u>sat</u> on the bench and <u>cheered</u> her team, the Rockets, against the visiting team, the Panthers. Earlier in the game, Louise, the star pitcher of the Rockets, <u>sprained</u> her arm in the opening pitch. Now, in the last inning with a one run Rockets advantage and bases loaded, her replacement, Jenny, also <u>sprained</u> her arm. In a desperate move, Dalia, the coach of the Rockets, <u>told</u> Tamara, "Try your best honey. Just try not to break your hand when you throw the ball."*

Example 2 reads much more smoothly because the tense is consistent. The last sentence contains a quotation which creates a situation where a shift to present tense is appropriate. Also consider the following example.

Example 3: *When the teacher said, "We will now turn to page 103," we all laughed because of the funny picture we knew was there.*

In this sentence, the shift in tense is clear and appropriate. The quotation marks the shift in tense, so it does not come as an unexpected surprise to the reader. Be sure to pay attention to verb tense in order to improve your writing.

Copyright © American Book Company

Shifts in Person

"Person" refers to the point of view of the writer, as outlined in the chart below.

Person	Point of View	Use Pronouns
first person	the writer speaks	*I* or *we*
second person	the writer speaks to the reader	*you*
third person	the writer speaks about someone or something	*he, she, it,* or *they*

Shifts in person have a similar effect to shifts in tense. They can cause confusion by making the reader unsure of the writer's perspective. Consider the following passage.

Example 3:   *When I saw the water bubbling up from the ground, I knew there was a pipe leaking under there. I started digging slowly because you never know if you might hit the pipe or an electrical cord. You just have to be careful. As I dug deeper, I found the leak. You can just imagine how happy I was to find it.*

In everyday speech, shifting from *I* to *you* is quite common. However, this practice does not follow the rules of written Standard American English. In Example 3, the writer tells a personal story about an underground water leak. The writer begins speaking from the perspective of the first person, then shifts to the second person, then back to first and finally, back to second. These shifts interfere with the clarity and flow of the passage. Compare the revised passage below.

Example 4:   *When I saw the water coming up from the ground, I knew there was a pipe leaking under there. I started digging slowly because I knew I might hit the pipe or an electrical cord. So, I dug carefully. As I dug deeper, I found the leak. I was very happy to find it.*

Example 4 gives the reader a clear sense of where the narrator stands in relation to the story. The narrator maintains the first person point of view, rather than shifting points of view.

> ***Keep person and tense consistent in your writing.***

PRACTICE 4: SHIFTS IN TENSE OR PERSON

Rewrite the following sentences, making sure that tense and person are consistent.

1.   A person who wants to learn how to play piano must be dedicated because you have to practice every day.

_____

_____

   Copyright © American Book Company

2. I was walking to the laundromat when I saw Philip, and I was talking with him.

   _____

   _____

3. A typical first-year student has trouble adjusting to a new schedule, but after a while, they learn their schedule.

   _____

   _____

4. I went to the post office to mail a letter, but I couldn't because you know how long the line gets.

   _____

   _____

5. One needs to take out huge loans before they can go to college.

   _____

   _____

6. It was the first of October, and I'm planning on driving into the mountains to see the leaves change color.

   _____

   _____

7. An athlete never knows when they might suffer an injury.

   _____

   _____

8. So many children go hungry every day, while other people threw food in the trash.

   _____

   _____

Copyright © American Book Company

9. People don't think it will happen to them, but a bad illness made them lose their job and home.

_____

_____

10. Because a growing baby is so small, any drugs a pregnant mother took affected the baby greatly.

_____

_____

CHECKING FOR PARALLEL SENTENCE STRUCTURE

Parallel sentence structure means that the parts of the sentence which are equally important are also similarly expressed. In other words, verbs match with verbs, adjectives with adjectives, prepositional phrases with prepositional phrases, and so on. Note the parallel structure in the following famous sentences.

> **I came; I saw; I conquered.**   **– Julius Ceasar**

> **Ask not what your country can do for you; ask what you can do for your country.**
>   **– John F. Kennedy**

> **For I was hungry and you gave me food; I was thirsty and you gave me something to drink; I was a stranger and you welcomed me.**   **– Jesus Christ**

These sentences have a rhythm and power because they are written in parallel structure. Writing that is not parallel can be difficult to read, and it is not Standard English. Read the following examples.

Not Parallel: *Billy knows how to play basketball, sing opera, and can even cook gourmet meals.*

Parallel: *Billy knows how to play basketball, sing opera, and cook gourmet meals.*

Not Parallel: *The three best things about summer are eating ice cream, swimming at the pool, and no school.*

Parallel: *The three best things about summer are eating ice cream, swimming at the pool, and not going to school.*

> *Parallel sentence structure means matching verbs with verbs, adjectives with adjectives, and so on.*

Copyright © American Book Company

PRACTICE 5: PARALLEL SENTENCE STRUCTURE

Rewrite the following sentences using parallel sentence structure.

1. The coach told us to go to bed early, to eat a good breakfast and don't arrive late for the game.

   _____

   _____

2. The school lunches need more fresh fruit, less fried food, and there should be more choices.

   _____

   _____

3. We searched for Sadie upstairs, downstairs, and crawled under the house.

   _____

   _____

4. My hobbies include reading books, watching movies, and stamp collecting.

   _____

   _____

5. In this class, we will learn to blend various colors, to use different types of paper, and how to draw realistic portraits.

   _____

   _____

6. Did you make your bed, wash your clothes, and cleaned your room today?

   _____

   _____

7. Statistics show that the world's population will increase rapidly while the world's resources are declining at an alarming rate.

   _____

   _____

Copyright © American Book Company

DEVELOPING SENTENCE VARIETY

Sentence variety involves writing sentences of different structures and lengths. It includes using different types of words and phrases. These variations make your writing more interesting to the reader. Three ways to develop sentence variety are by **combining simple sentences into longer ones**, **starting a sentence with something other than the subject**, and **using a question or exclamation occasionally**.

Combining Simple Sentences

Simple, direct sentences are often the best way to convey ideas. However, if these simple sentences become repetitive, they make the writing uninteresting. Compare the two examples below.

Example 1:   *We went to the basketball game. We were late. There was a huge crowd of cheering fans. The team won. Everybody celebrated in the parking lot. Then, some jubilant fans had parties at their houses. It was a great night.*

Example 2:   *After arriving late to the basketball game, we joined the huge crowd in cheering our team to victory. Hundreds of people continued the celebration into the parking lot and then on to the homes of jubilant fans. What a night!*

Example 1 is a list of simple sentences, and the repetition is boring. In Example 2, the writer has combined several of these simple sentences into a few longer ones. Both passages tell the same story, but the second one is more interesting to read because of sentence variety.

Starting the Sentence with Different Beginnings

Most sentences begin with a subject, continue with a verb, and end with an object. Adjectives and adverbs may appear along the way. This pattern works well as long as your writing doesn't get repetitive and boring. Therefore, from time to time, start a sentence with something other than the subject. Look at the following examples:

Begin with an adverb:
Replace "I found myself suddenly in a bad situation." with
"<u>Suddenly</u>, I found myself in a bad situation."

Begin with a prepositional phrase:
Replace "We stopped at the ice cream stand on the way home." with
"<u>On the way home</u>, we stopped at the ice cream stand."

Begin with a participial phrase:
Replace "The children ran into the candy store, screaming with joy." with
"<u>Screaming with joy</u>, the children ran into the candy store."

The examples above show different ways of forming sentences. They also show how a modifier is best understood when it is placed near the noun or verb it is modifying.

Copyright © American Book Company

Using a Question or Exclamation

Finally, using a **question** or **exclamation** occasionally can provide a welcome change of pace for the reader. Compare the following two examples:

Example 3: *I didn't like it when my best friend told me he was going out with my ex-girlfriend. It was the worst feeling I've ever experienced.*

Example 4: *How would you like it if your best friend told you he was going out with your ex-girlfriend? Well, I know. It's the worst feeling I've ever experienced!*

Examples 3 and 4 show how to use a question or exclamation to add variety to your writing. Example 4 also shows how a shift in person can be used effectively.

> *Vary your sentences by combining simple sentences into longer ones, starting a sentence with something other than the subject, and using a question or exclamation occasionally.*

PRACTICE 6: SENTENCE VARIETY

Rewrite the following paragraphs by varying the sentences.

1.   My friends and I went to Phillips Arena to see professional wrestling. There was a huge crowd. Everybody was screaming and yelling. All the fans were cheering for their favorite wrestlers. My favorite wrestler won all her matches. She flipped one of her opponents off the mat. She flew into the crowd. I was scared that she was going to land on me. She fell right next to me. I saw her up close. I saw that she was very big.

2.   My best friend is a guy. We've known each other forever. Other girls ask me about him. They ask me why we are good friends. I tell them he is funny. He thinks of weird stuff. He tells me this stuff to hear me laugh. Sometimes I just tell him that he is too strange. He will listen to my opinion. He says that he is glad that he knows someone who will both laugh and tell him different.

3.   You never know what effect you can have on other people. Sometimes it can be a big effect. Our school held a talent show. My friends and I did a lip sync to the old Madonna song, "Like a Prayer." The crowd cheered. Everyone thought it was great. After the show, everyone wanted to tell us how great we were. I shook everybody's hand. I had a little fever that day. I found out later that I had strep throat. A lot of students were out sick the next week.

4.   There's a new student in our school. His name is Omar. Most of his friends are in the chess club. He wasn't very popular. He wanted to run for student council. There was another student who was coming up for re-election. Her name is Theresa. Omar's friends were excited about his campaign. They put up a lot of posters all around the school. Omar gave a good speech. He had some good ideas. This was the first time he did something like this. He won by a small margin.

PRACTICE 7: REVISING

A. **Based on the skills you learned in this chapter, revise the following paragraphs.**

1.   The first and primary duty and responsibility of an American citizen is to support and uphold the government, the United States, and the Congress. In particular, a citizen can become a member of the local school board. I enjoy eating that old American favorite, the hot dog. You could be an active part of public education. You could influence the lives of children in your community. Another way to support the government is to serve on a jury in a public trial. We could keep criminals out of society. You must be an active citizen. Then our government will be stronger because of the active participation and involvement of all citizens.

2.   At first, do not be scared when people in public tried to communicate with you. We Americans are much more outgoing than I saw in Britain. They are the kind of people who are more subdued. They put smile on their face that is polite. People were very emotional here in the United States. When Americans are happy and cheerful, they will show it. When they are unhappy and sad, they are not embarrassed to cry in front of the other many people.

3.   Becoming popular in life has one big part of people getting into groups. To become popular may cause a person to join a group because they want to prove themselves to someone. This happens usually to new students at a new school. Becoming popular and well-known in the working area is about the same as school. This happens when someone gets a job they would like to keep. They try to impress the boss. People also join groups to become popular to be cool, so other people around them will like them.

B. **Return to Practice 13: Writing the Draft, on page 98 in Chapter 4. In this practice exercise, you wrote several essays on various topics. Based on what you have learned in Chapter 5, revise these essays to make them better. Then, share your essays with other students, seek their input, and incorporate their suggestions to improve your essays.**

Use the following checklist to help you.

☐ I added clarifying information.

☐ I corrected any shifts in tense or person.

☐ I deleted any unrelated sentences.

☐ I checked for parallel sentence structure.

☐ I eliminated any unnecessary words.

☐ I used sentences of different lengths and structures.

Note: You will proofread these essays in Chapter 6: Proofreading the Essay.

Copyright © American Book Company

CHAPTER 5 SUMMARY: REVISING THE ESSAY

- *Make sure you provide the audience with enough information to understand your ideas.*

- *Delete sentences or phrases that are not directly related to the paragraph or essay.*

- *Good writing expresses ideas clearly through effective words–the fewer the better.*

- *Keep person and tense consistent in your writing.*

- *Parallel sentence structure means matching verbs with verbs, adjectives with adjectives, and so on.*

- *Vary your sentences by combining simple sentences into longer ones, starting a sentence with something other than the subject, and using a question or exclamation occasionally.*

Copyright © American Book Company

CHAPTER 5 REVIEW: REVISING THE ESSAY

A.   **Using the skills you practiced in this chapter, revise the essay below. It was written as a response to the following writing prompt.**

Writing Situation

   You arrive at the school counselor's office to decide what kind of classes you wish to take. The counselor turns to you and says, "You should take classes which will be aligned with what kind of career or school you want to enter upon graduation. What career do you see for yourself?"

Directions for Writing

   Write a letter to your school counselor explaining what field you wish to enter and why you have chosen that field. Include details and convincing information to show your counselor that you are serious about your career choice.

Dear Counselor Billings,

   I would like to show you why I am now choosing to pursue a medical career.   While I have been growing up I have had many doctors to inspire me. When I was diagnosed with cancer as a young four-year-old, I was very scared. However, the doctors and nurses took the time to explain how they would help me. In the end I would like to be a doctor to help others in an important way, provide an income for my family, and make important contributions to the medical field.

   Most importantly, I want to be in a profession where I can help people in the way I was helped. Being a doctor would give me the ability to touch the lives of people because being there for some one when their health is at risk and being able to give them the advice they need is a great feeling. I look forward to looking at my patients as people. not cases. I want to make them laugh, as well as give them the medicine they need. I want to make their lives better by giving them real support and lending them my expertise. The best kind of knowledge to have is the kind that you can share with the world.

   Secondly, providing an income for the family I will have one day concerns me. I don't want to have to work sixty hours a week in a job I hate so that I can bring in enough money, to keep my family taken care of. I want to have time to spend with my family instead of being with a company that becomes my family because I spend so much time there. I want to be able to earn enough in a regular work-week to not need to work overtime hours. Being a doctor will give me the opportunity to work the hours I want while still being able to provide for my family.

   Thirdly, I want to pursue a career in medicine so that one day I can make important discoveries to help patients. I believe there are other cures to cancers waiting out there in the world. I find it hard to believe that the only way today to cure people from cancer is to inject them with poisonous chemicals. I was really scared when I was a kid and all my hair fell out. Those chemicals do things to your body that nature didn't intend. Aand they damage you. I want to find cures for diseases from the natural world. Our bodies are natural, so we shouldn't be surprised to find cures for diseases coming from nature. I would like to be at the front of efforts to find natural remedies to many of the diseases afflicting the people.

Copyright © American Book Company

To tell you the truth, I want to be a doctor because I can help people in an important way, provide a good income for my future family without having to work too hard, and contribute mportant natural discoveries for cures for diseases. Being able to work my own hours will help have balance between future family responsiblities and work. Helping people is why I feel I have been put on this earth, and I want to help someone in the way someone else helped me. In addition, producing natural cures for diseases will help me to leave this earth feeling I have made a lasting difference while I was here.

Sincerely,

Felix Lee

B.   **For the Review in Chapter 4: Drafting the Essay, you wrote drafts for several different essays based on your prewriting activities from Chapter 3: Planning the Essay. Return to those essays now. Revise them based on the skills you practiced in this chapter. You may also use the checklist below which is reproduced from page 116.**

- ☐ I added clarifying information.

- ☐ I corrected any shifts in tense or person.

- ☐ I deleted any unrelated sentences.

- ☐ I checked for parallel sentence structure.

- ☐ I eliminated any unnecessary words.

- ☐ I used sentences of different lengths and structures.

Note: You will proofread these essays in the Chapter 6 Review, so keep them in your writing folder.

Copyright © American Book Company

ADDITIONAL ACTIVITIES: REVISING THE ESSAY

1.   Revise the essay below. It was written in response to the following writing prompt.

Writing Situation

   You are a journalist for your school newspaper. Your school is considering whether to require all people entering the school to pass through a metal detector. Violence has been on the rise on campus, but no one has yet been caught using a weapon. Some people think it's a good idea to increase safety at your school. Others think it's an invasion of privacy. The editor has asked you to write an editorial for the school newspaper describing your feelings on this issue to the student body.

Directions for Writing

   Write an editorial stating your position on the introduction of metal detectors at your school. Use convincing arguments to persuade your readers to agree with you.

Now that the year is winding down, we be confronting an important issue. Do we want metal detectors in our school next year or not? This issue is complex because, you know, we have had a lot of problems with student violence on campus. At this moment anyone can walk on campus with a knife or gun in their pocket and no one would know until the person decided to display or use the weapon. At the same time, having metal detectors inhibits our freedom. Every time we want to enter the school would be having to submit to an electronic search. I believe however that the benefits of having metal detectors far outweigh the costs. Every time we have something metallic on, we will have to remove it and display it to the public. This interferes with our constitutional right to privacy. We need to protect ourselves from our own student body and from visitors to campus in order to make the school a truly safe environment.

   Firstly, the metal detectors will protect us from ourselves. As students, we know how easy it is for us to get our emotions up on any number of issues. It doesn't take much arguments be starting all of the time over boyfriends and girlfriends. More often than not on campus these days, students be fighting about these problems instead of discussing them. Another thing, people starting vicious rumors cause people to get angry. We have had two people on campus arrested already for assault and battery in separate incidents. As violence increases, the numbers show that the potential for weapons to come into play be increasing to. Weapons, unlike a fist, has a much higher potential to permanently disable or kill. Weapons be causing all kinds of tragedy among the student body. Needless to say, I understand how students would feel hassled by going through machines and having to remove metallic items because some of you people will probably need to change your whole wardrobe! However, students need to realize it is for their own safety that this is becoming necessary.

   Secondly, metal detectors will protect us from visitors that may want to harm us on campus. Currently, people may come on campus with the permission of the administration, but they do not get searched for weapons beforehand. Let's say some intelligent, crazy person convinces to administration to let him on campus for show and tell or something, then he pulls

Copyright © American Book Company

out a handgun while we're changing classes and kills ten of us. Now who here wants that. No one of course. If visitors get offended about being having to go through a metal detector, maybe they have something to hide.

To make it short, the safety of the student body, visitors, and the school faculty is at stake in this decision. We need to complete our education in a safe environment for all, so please support the installation of metal detectors starting next fall.

2. You are entering a contest to win a new Lexus convertible. You must write an essay that addresses the following question: "Who is your all-time favorite entertainer?" Brainstorm about this topic, and write your draft. Try to convince the judges that your choice is the best one. Then, use the skills you learned in this chapter to revise you essay. Share the essay with the class or with your instructor.

3. One of your friends lies about everything from how much money his family has to all of the parties he goes to every weekend. Persuade him that lying is wrong and will hurt him in the long run. Do prewriting activities (brainstorming, freewriting, clustering, outlining) on this topic. Then, write a draft for an essay. Revise this essay based on the tips and strategies you practiced in this chapter. Compare your revision with those of others in the class.

4. With a partner or in a small group, exchange your essays from number 1 or 2 above. Provide oral or written feedback to each other. Use the checklist on page 116 as a guide. If you agree with your peers, incorporate their suggestions into an improved revision of your essay. Then, share it with the class or with your teacher.

Chapter 6
Proofreading the Essay

Your essay has been written and revised, and now it is ready for scoring, right?
Well, it is almost ready, but not even the best writers turn in a piece of writing
before they do a careful **proofreading**. Proofreading is the process of checking
your essay for errors in capitalization, punctuation, spelling, and grammar as well
as for repeated words or omitted words. Before turning in your final copy, take
time to look for these small, but important, errors.

The Georgia High School Writing Test requires you to demonstrate knowledge of
Standard American English through grammar and usage, punctuation, and sentence formation.
Proofreading the final copy of your essay will help you demonstrate these skills. In this chapter,
you will review proofreading notation, and then practice proofreading for errors in the following
areas of writing:

- **Capitalization**
- **Internal Punctuation**
- **Grammar and Usage**
- **Spelling**
- **Sentence Formation**

If you or your teacher feels more practice or review of grammar would be beneficial, read
the text and complete the exercises in American Book Company's companion resources, *Basics
Made Easy: Grammar & Usage Review* or *Basics Made Easy: Grammar & Usage* software.

PROOFREADING NOTATION

Handwriting is not graded on the Georgia High School Writing Test, but if your paper cannot be
read, it will not be graded. So, write neatly and clearly even for your proofreading corrections.
Proofreading notation refers to certain ways of making corrections that are standard among
writers. Below is an example of how you might make corrections to the third paragraph from
the essay about the effects of children watching television (on page 103).

Commercials are another problem with television. As well as advertising shows with

adult content, commercials persuade children to buy products theat they do not need. Thats   That is

how television pays for itself: Companies pay to put commercials on television and they hope   c

children will buy there stuff. The voice on commercials tell children that they will be happy if   their   s

they buy a certain toy or cereal. They will be like other children, And other children will like   a

them if they have those products. It is difficult enough for adults to tell the difference between

reality fiction in commercials. How are a three-year-old supposed to do that?   and   is

Copyright © American Book Company

Notice how the proofreading marks are written neatly and clearly so that they do not interfere with reading the passage. Develop standard abbreviations and notations for editing your writing. Though you do not necessarily need to use these standard markings on the Georgia High School Writing Test, your teacher may use them for evaluating practice essays.

EDITING AND PROOFREADING CHART

Symbol	Meaning	Example
sp	spelling error	Their back from vacation. (sp)
cap	capitalization error	I live in the north, but my sister lives in the south. (cap)
. ? !	end marks	Where are you going. (?)
,	comma	Hello Mr. Ripley (,)
^	add	Ray went to ^ the store.
/	change	Television teaches ~~kids~~ children manners
frag	fragment	Near Kokomo. (frag)
RO	run-on	He tripped, he fell. (RO)
t	tense error	Yesterday I walk to school. (t)
s-v	subject-verb agreement	Keisha and I loves to shop. (s-v)
mod	misplaced modifier	Quickly, Sam ate the sandwich. (mod)

Standard proofreading notation is not necessary for the Georgia High School Writing Test, but make your corrections neatly and clearly, so that the graders can easily read your essay.

CAPITALIZATION

Capitalization involves the practice of using a mixture of capital letters ("A") and lower case letters ("a"). In the early development of English, writers used only capital letters. Now, in modern English, there are rules for capitalizing certain words in order to emphasize their importance. One example is the first word of a sentence, like the word "**One**" which began this sentence. Another example of words that are capitalized is proper nouns, like "Georgia." There are many other examples of times when a word should be capitalized. Think for a moment about the examples which you know.

Looking for errors in capitalization is an important proofreading skill. You will practice this skill in the following exercise.

> *Certain words are capitalized to emphasize their importance. These words include the first word in a sentence, proper nouns, and many other examples.*

PRACTICE 1: CAPITALIZATION

Carefully read the letter below, proofreading for errors in capitalization. (Circle) all of the words with capitalization errors, including words that should have been capitalized and were not, as well as words which should *not* have been capitalized but were. *Hint:* There are forty-eight (48) words with capitalization errors to find.

july 24, 2007

dear mr. Golden,

My Family and i finally went on our vacation to the grand canyon in arizona. we got there on a Wednesday Morning. My brother, will, and I both wanted to go on the Helicopter tour first, but mom and dad said–"Later!"

When we first walked to the Edge of the South Rim, our jaws dropped, and we exclaimed "oh, wow!" at one time. Mom took a step back. "oh," She said, "I don't think I can hike this!

Some german Tourists, hearing our english voices, stopped by us at that moment to ask about the horseback tours. We helped them find the Camp office, and we spoke with kelly o'hara, the Park Ranger on duty. after giving us information about the Canyon and reassuring Mom about the bright angel Trail, Ranger o'hara asked if we were from the south. I guess our accents are more noticeable than i had thought . . .

Since I know that you, as my english Professor, will be asking for this later, Maybe you could look over my Outline for the Annual "what I did this summer" paper.

    I.   Memorial day pool Visit

       A.   sunburn

          1.   Second degree burns

                      sincerely yours,

                      Leigh Harpar

INTERNAL PUNCTUATION

Internal Punctuation refers to the writing marks that are used within the structure of a sentence. They include **commas**, **colons**, **semi-colons**, **apostrophes**, and **quotation marks**. The appropriate use of these marks adds clarity and logic to your writing.

Copyright © American Book Company

Commas ,

The action of writing an essay has a certain flow and thought process in drafting and even in revising. This flow can create an engaging paper, but it can also lead to omissions of certain punctuation. **Commas** are often forgotten in the flow of writing. Proofreading for any missing commas is important for the clarity of your paper.

Commas can signal a contrast, set off extra information, or separate items in lists. There are other uses for commas as well. Consider what you know about using commas, and then begin the next exercise.

PRACTICE 2: COMMAS

Read the story below carefully, looking for all missing commas. Insert commas where they are needed, and (circle) them. *Hint:* **There are thirty-five (35) commas that are missing.**

What's in a Car's Name?

In our college library I fingered the book's jacket in disbelief. The title had to be a joke or was it? The letters stood out lemon yellow on a cobalt blue background spelling out the words "How To Name Your Car." I told my best friend Renatta "Hey look at this!"

"Well yeah" she remarked in a bored tone "I saw a poem like that in my lit class by T. S. Eliot about how to name your cat. Crazy huh?" Still curious I headed to the nearest table to find out why this book would have been written and what it said.

When I began reading the book I realized that it detailed not only car names but also who would choose to name a car. Apparently Southerners who have not gone past the high school level in their education are more likely than other people to name their vehicles especially their mud-caked trucks and open-air jeeps. Sitting at that table I felt my past revealed exposed. My parents with their two semesters of college between them had named our huge maroon station wagon "Battle Axe." It was a righteous and well-deserved title. My family also according to the book fell into the common masses category by referring to this hulking machine with the pronoun "she." In her glory days she plowed into several smaller cars–usually in the shopping center parking lot where my mother vainly tried to overcome the "blind spot" that came with the car. Battle Axe always came away unscarred from the crashes but the other cars weren't so lucky.

After fourteen years we got our next car on May 17 1988. This new "she" had been pre-owned by my grandparents who lived in Baltimore Maryland. She was a pale yellow black-topped Chevelle with a sweet 350 engine–she could move out! What did we name her? We named her "Cream Puff." She and her name lasted until the puff from her engine became a black oily cloud of smoke.

For myself I have named cars; however with my college experience it seems as if I don't have enough sense to remember to use the names and the cars don't last as long. I've used the names "Blue Meanie" "Behemoth" and "W. G." or "Wise Guy"–HE was quite a car. This soon-to-graduate Southern female has at least broken through the sexist mold when naming her cars.

Copyright © American Book Company

Colons : Semi-colons ; and Apostrophes ,

The **colon** signals that there is a bit of information that the sentence needs. It most often sets off a list, a quotation, an appositive (renaming), an explanation, or an example. Colons are also used in number phrases such as time notation or Biblical references. Two major rules about the colon are

1) <u>never</u> place it right after a verb (between the verb and its object), and
2) <u>never</u> use it to separate two independent clauses with a coordinating conjunction between them.

You may use a **semi-colon** to separate two independent clauses that are closely related to one idea. (For more emphasis, you may also use a colon in this case, especially to emphasize the second clause.) Another common use of the semi-colon is to separate items in a list when the item names contain commas.

Apostrophes do not separate anything; they signal either possession or missing letters in contractions.

To improve your proofreading skill, consider the guidelines above and consider how you normally use these punctuation marks. Then complete the following exercise.

PRACTICE 3: COLONS, SEMI-COLONS, AND APOSTROPHES

Carefully read the following story (it continues to the next page), first for content. Next, insert the missing punctuation marks, and (circle) them. *Hint:* **There are twenty-four (24) colons, semi-colons, and apostrophes (signaling omitted letters) missing in the passage.**

Wild Life Unleashed!

Wildlife, exotic wildlife, is moving into a neighborhood near you, according to these news stories a five-foot iguana, sunning herself on a rock, startled kids at a local elementary school a large python, an abandoned pet, was found inside the mayors limo, digesting a meal and the Humane Society was called to trap piranhas that were eating rare koi fish in a park pond.

Where does this exotic wildlife come from? It is imported by people who see exotic pet ownership as cool whereas, its really quite brutal. Even in the 70s, the United States experienced a craze in wild animal ownership, promoting the importation of exotic wildlife including the following ocelots, cheetahs, and Canadian wolves. The rich and famous paraded these animals with rhinestone collars and leashes down city streets. The craze lasted until the animals matured and reverted to wild habits howling at all hours, spraying walls, and shredding the owners' belongings. Reports of cruelty and neglect increased, and zoos refused to take these animals for lack of space and the high level of nursing they required. The federal customs agency mercifully stepped in, halting the importation of these wild creatures.

Copyright © American Book Company

Nowadays, the exotic pet of choice is more likely to be a reptile or a carnivorous fish of some kind. Parents buy or allow their children to buy these creatures, believing them to be ideal companions quiet, caged, and low-maintenance. When the pets have grown too large or too worrisome, however, theyre dumped into rural areas, including local waterways, to fend for themselves.

The following letter is a possible scenario illustrating the hazards of exotic pets

Gilbert's Trout Farm

Dear Sir

I m writing to let you know about some stuff that I think I lost in your lake. On September 2, 2007, at 7 27 a. m., I was fishing with my parents when I lost the following things a flashlight, with extra batteries two rock n roll covers for CDs with tubes of Virtualglu taped inside and a fresh water eel, with huge teeth. Its cage is missing too. I am sorry for the trouble, but my family is ok with the eel being gone.

Sincerely,
Will Stephens

This accidental release of a wild pet is an exception it is usually done intentionally. The zoos and nature centers are again refusing to take the new form of exotic pets, and these animals are taken either to vets to be put to death or to remote areas to be abandoned. In the text of the Old Testament, Genesis 1 28, humans are given dominion over the other creatures on Earth. Isnt it time to consider a more humane philosophy of dominion where there is nurturing and care, instead of exploitation and neglectful ownership?

Beware! The next wave of released pets will be even smaller life forms fuzzy tarantulas, desert scorpions, and Madagascar hissing cockroaches. Dont give in to the lure of this bizarre form of consumerism. You might end up just being bugged.

Quotation Marks   " "

Quotation marks are signals that frame words belonging to someone other than the author. When used in fiction, quotation marks help to keep the voices of different characters from becoming confused. There are two types of quotation marks:

double quotation marks (" ") are used to signal direct quotes or some titles
single quotation marks (' ') are used to signal quotes within quotes

Copyright © American Book Company

PRACTICE 4: QUOTATION MARKS

Carefully read the story on this page, first for content. Then, look for missing quotation marks, and add the quotation marks where needed. Next, circle the ones you added. *Hint:* **There are nine (9) pairs of double " " marks and one (1) pair of single ' ' marks missing.**

Summer Blight

Race you to that mimosa! challenged Sophie, pointing to a slender pink-dotted tree.

You're on, dork, snorted Terrell, and the loser has to bring everybody colas.

They took off, with me—dead last as usual. We fell under the scant shade of the tree, panting and sweating from the summer's heat. I rolled onto my back to look up through the mimosa's fern-like leaves.

Did y'all know that these trees were all killed by a blight years back? I asked. My aunt Beryl always talks about climbing these trees as a kid, but they were huge then. Now the blight is over, and the mimosas are growing again, but they're all scrawny, like this'n here. I wonder when they'll be big enough to be good climbing trees again . . .

Sophie sat up, frowning and fussing, Don't try to change the subject. You know it's you that's got to get the drinks, and while you're at it, you might as well bring food, too.

Terrell agreed with her (as usual) that, as the fartherest-back-of-all-time loser, I should bring anything they wanted. My speech had backfired—making them hungrier and thirstier than ever. I tried again.

With this drought goin' on, the worst in history even, I think we should forgit the drinks. Just remember, I said raising a hand into the air, that wise Southern saying, Don't spit; you might need it. And I think . . .

Sophie and Terrell threw dust, thistles, and rude names at me until I got up and trudged off, feeling as much a loser as Charlie Brown in the comic strip Peanuts. But, as I got closer to our screened door, I started daydreaming about what would happen if I fell in a hole or was taken by aliens. Sophie and Terrell—well, I expect that both of them would just wither up and blow away like blighted mimosa shoots.

> *Use appropriate internal punctuation within your sentences, including commas, colons, semi-colons, apostrophes, and quotation marks.*

Copyright © American Book Company

GRAMMAR AND USAGE

Grammar and usage refers to the ways that writers put together words, phrases, sentences, and paragraphs. When you are proofreading, you want to make sure that you have followed the rules for Standard American English. Look for mistakes in your usage of **nouns**, **articles**, **adjectives**, **adverbs**, **negative words**, **verbs**, and **subject-verb agreement**.

Nouns and Articles

Nouns are words which name people, places, things, ideas, and concepts. **Common nouns** name general examples of these. **Proper nouns** name specific people, places, things, ideas, and concepts and are capitalized. Proper nouns are capitalized and common nouns are not. There is a special group of nouns called collective nouns. **Collective nouns** name single units made up of many members. Two examples are a **school** of fish and a **committee** of delegates.

Nouns may be **possessive**, showing ownership or a relationship. There are several different ways to form the possessive of a noun. Two of the guidelines are as follows: for a singular noun, add an **'s**; if the noun is plural and ends in <u>s</u>, then add only an apostrophe after the letter <u>s</u>.

In English, **articles** like "the" or "a" are closely associated with nouns. These small words often give the reader essential information about the noun they accompany. There are three forms of articles:

      definite–"the"   **indefinite–"a / an"**   **zero–no article**

1.   The first form, the **definite article**, is "the." It can be used with any type of noun. **"The"** marks a thing that is known to readers either by general knowledge, the context of the rest of the writing, or by the information in the noun phrase.

    Example 1:   **The** sun rises in the morning.
    Example 2:   A wildfire blazed out of control in eastern Colorado. It is **the** worst fire seen in 200 years.
    Example 3:   **the** hills of Tennessee, *or*
                     the blizzard that shut down Atlanta in 1993

There are three instances where "the" is always needed:
- Before the word <u>same</u> (**the same** time zone)
- Generally before a written (ordinal) number (**the first** star I see)
- Before a superlative statement (**the best** music)

2.   The second form, the **indefinite article**, <u>a / an</u>, does not identify a certain thing. The writer may know of the particular noun item but does not expect the reader to know it. The indefinite article <u>a / an</u> can only be used with singular nouns. The article <u>a</u> is used before a word that begins with a consonant letter or sound. The article <u>an</u> is used before words that begin with a vowel letter or sound.
    Example 1:   I went to <u>a</u> <u>c</u>oncert.   He worked on <u>a</u> <u>r</u>ailroad.
    Example 2:   She had <u>an</u> <u>e</u>gg for breakfast.   They drove for <u>an</u> <u>h</u>our to get to the fair.

Copyright © American Book Company

3.	The third form, the **zero article**, means no article at all. No articles are used with plural or uncounted nouns. Often, generalizations are made with no article.

Example 1:	We will serve **hot tea** with lunch.
Example 2:	**Trees** give off oxygen, benefitting our atmosphere.
Example 3:	Religious texts are founded on **faith**.

PRACTICE 5: NOUNS AND ARTICLES

The following news review involves practice for nouns and articles. Read it carefully, and follow the directions for each part.

Part A:	In LINES 1-7 ONLY, look for nouns and articles. Underline all <u>common nouns</u> once, underline all <u>proper nouns</u> twice, and (circle) all articles. *Hint:* There are twenty-four (24) common nouns, three (3) proper nouns, and thirteen (13) articles.

Not the Same Old Grind!

1	Have you been to the new skateboard park? If not, you've got to go. It's so awesome! It's
2	called Skateboard Survivor Park. The entire complex is arranged so skateboarders have
3	the right-of-way. The park's property is a sprawling 27 acres of convenient urban land.
4	The park's compassionate leader is J. C. Powell, a life-long educator. Mr. Powell's vision
5	for the park was that it be a safe but challenging course for serious skateboarders. After
6	only a few crises, construction was completed on schedule. The master-of-ceremonies
7	speech was made on skateboards; an official showed off the park's unique features. There
8	are grinding railes, half-pipes, rampies, multi-level shelfs and spirals for extreme speed and
9	complicated maneuvers. Previewing the park, I saw some skateboarderes shooting around
10	like torpedos and others bailing out like dominois. A brand new skateboarding splash
11	fountain works great for cooling off and jumping off. The huge food court, three storys
12	high, can be reached by avenuess that are marked "Skateboard Traffic Only." When has
13	that been seen before? The walking crowd has its own pathwaies and food kioskes: set
14	around the perimeter of park only. The best wayes to reach the park include city busis
15	and the underground rail system. There is a small entrance fee that gives you run of the
16	parks' grounds for as long as you can survive or until they vote you out at closing time. I
17	don't know about you, but I'm voting to grab my boards' and head over there right now!

Part B:	In LINES 8-17, look for incorrectly written possessive and plural nouns and missing articles. Neatly strike through the incorrect form, and clearly write the correct form above it. For missing articles, use the caret sign, ^ , and supply the missing word. *Hint:* There are sixteen (16) errors.

	Copyright © American Book Company

Pronouns

Pronouns take the place of nouns in a sentence. A pronoun must agree in number and gender with the noun it replaces. Some examples of pronouns are **I, you, she, he, it, we, they, us, their, who, that, someone, whose, none,** and **nobody.** Some of these pronouns may act as adjectives when they are followed by a noun: for example, **that, those,** or **these.** Also, there are pronouns which may begin a question: for example, **what, who,** or **whose.**

Before beginning the next practice, you may want to consider how you use pronouns or review the use of pronouns in the companion text, American Book Company's *Basics Made Easy: Grammar and Usage.*

PRACTICE 6: PRONOUNS

Read the following essay carefully, first for content. (Note that it continues onto the next page.) After reading the passage, go back and read the directions for Parts A and B.

Part A: **In this section, find and (circle) the pronouns.** *Hint:* **There are eighteen (18) pronouns used in this section.**

Playground of Impressions

Once upon a time, say in second grade, two kids meet on a playground for the first time, and if they don't beat each other up, then a friendship grows. Those innocent days pass quickly, however, and soon these same kids learn to be more wary of how they react in social situations. Even young children begin to use a "Public Face." These two kids could be you and me or anyone we know. Everyone has some type of mask that they use in social settings to protect their private selves from ridicule, whether it, the ridicule, is real or imagined. Often a destructive mind-set of "us against them" can develop when people bond in this shallow, appearances-only, type of way. So the question is should I, or should you, trust and act upon first impressions? No, we should not. It is better for us to let a friendship grow with the passing of a few seasons.

Part B: **In this section, proofread for errors in pronoun usage. Strike through the errors that you find, neatly, and then write the correct pronoun form above each error.** *Hint:* **There are 21 errors in pronoun usage.**

In a first impression, the brassiest personality may mask a shy, unsure self, and a quiet, dignified approach may only be covering up a really boring personality. You can see that there are many aspects to creating a first impression, but it are all based on surface appearance. There is the tilt of the head: is the person that I are meeting looking alert, confident, interested? They may indicate only a stiff neck instead of the proud carriage that us perceive. There is the impression of eye contact to be assessed: does this person look you in the eye with steady reassuring gazes? Them could really be the peering looks of a near-sighted person whose is trying to figure out just who I are. There is the tone of the voice: is this person speaking in a pleasant tone with an elegant accent? That person could really be pretentious and smothering a God-given accent or this poor soul could be trying to disguise a sinus condition. Lastly, there is a general message sent through clothing: are the clothes, who wearer is a stranger to them, the latest fashion and worn with flair and poise? That person could be employed by the mall department store and is a walking commercial or is a person so clothes-conscious that any one else's clothes are good enough to appreciate.

All of the above positive first looks were something my best friend in high school had. Them who met she for the first time admired her beauty and dignified ways. What them did not know was that her tried to commit suicide twice before graduation. Beauty did not protect this lovely girl from emotional problems. There was also in my high school a popular football player what had all of the best first looks. However, his was taking "legal" steroids which unfortunately affected him personality; they made him act violently. Many people were hurt whose were taken in by the first impression he demonstrated.

The image that began this discussion was a playground. The playground must be expanded as us grow. We must meet people in different situations over time to begin to understand who them are and if we should put in the time and effort of building a relationship with they. Remember: First impressions are the worst impressions.

Adjectives, Adverbs, and Negative Words

Adjectives are words that modify, or describe, nouns and pronouns. Adjectives answer the questions **Which? How many?** or **What kind?** In contrast to many other languages, English almost always places adjectives <u>before</u> the word(s) that they modify. **Pronouns** and **articles** can also function as adjectives.

Adverbs are used to modify many different kinds of words. Adverbs can modify verbs, adjectives, or other adverbs. Frequently, adverbs end in **-ly**, but not always. All adverbs answer one of these questions: **Where? When? In what manner?** or **To what extent?**

Adjectives and adverbs are also used to compare or "weigh" differences. The **comparative** form of adjectives and adverbs (**-er**) is used to compare two things. The **superlative** form of adjectives and adverbs (**-est**) is used to compare three or more things.

> **Note:** For words with one syllable, use the **-er** and **-est** ending. For words with two or more syllables, place **more**, **most**, **less**, or **least** in front of the comparing adjective or adverb. If the comparison is negative, use the words **worse** (two things) or **worst** (three or more things).

Copyright © American Book Company

Two **negative words** cannot be used to express one negative idea. When they are, it is called a **double negative**. Unfortunately, it is one of the most common errors in English: for example, *I can't hardly wait for summer vacation.* There are many negative words including **nothing**, **not**, **nearly**, **never**, **hardly**, **neither**, and **no one**.

PRACTICE 7: ADJECTIVES, ADVERBS, AND NEGATIVE WORDS

Read the following story for content. Then, proofread the text for correct use of adjectives, adverbs, and negative words. When you find an error, neatly strike through the word, and clearly write the correct form above it. *Hint:* There are thirty (30) errors.

Cake Walk

Kelly had waited eager for months before her sixteenth birthday party. Her mother promised to hold a dance party for her at the newer city community center, which was only one block from theirs apartment. Kelly's wholest family was going to be there as well as her tenth grade class. Aunt Marilyn, the more creative person in the large family, worked as the top cake decorator in Olgetree's Grocery, the better shop in the tri-city area. She came over weeks early to ask Kelly what cake she would like for this specialer party.

"I want two cakes," Kelly declared bold. "The firstest one is for all the girls. We want a Black Forest cake. You know the one with, like, red stuff inside and the deliciousest white icing."

"I know which one you mean," her aunt replied, smiling. "Do you know how the Black Forest cake got those name?"

"Uh, no," Kelly answered vague, thinking about the next cake she wanted.

Her aunt went on happy. "Well, it came from Germany, which has the deeper and dark forests in all of Europe. The "red stuff" is really chocolate cake. The most old legends of wood sprites say that woodland spirits brought the cake to a powerful king as a peace offering. The king, however, refused the cake, and the sprites cursed him. They say that there is still magic in the most old recipes of the Black Forest cake."

Copyright © American Book Company

Kelly shook her head, saying, "I don't never believe in that kind of stuff, Aunt Marilyn, but that was a great story. Now about the next cake. It will be for all the guys. Make it a Devil's Food cake."

"Girl!" her aunt exclaimed. "Are you trying to make trouble?"

"Just kidding!" Kelly laughed. "I really want the kind of cake that my bestest friend likes a lot. He likes a double-fudge chocolate cake with chocolate chunks and the more bigger the better."

The cakes were baked, and the night of the party arrived with the worstest blizzard that anyone had ever seen. There was even lightning and thunder with the huge snowfall. In the dance room, however, there was a ton of food, a greater band, and beautiful decorations. The time for cake came, and the lights were turned out. Kelly stood by Aunt Marilyn who held the cake, and everyone sang. Sudden, there was a tremendous crash of thunder and a blinding flash of light. The vibration was enough to start the cake sliding, with all sixteen candles burning, off the plate. It landed with a mournful squish–upside down. There was the more horriblest silence for three seconds, and then Aunt Marilyn tipped the cake more or less back on the plate, exclaiming, "Whatever you wished for will come true! Kelly, all the candles are out . . ."

But there was no Kelly. Someone whispered that she must have wished to disappear in the worstest way. Aunt Marilyn thought wild about the curse of the wood sprites. Then, the lights came back on, and Kelly was standing at the threshold with the second cake firm in her hands and a smile on her face that was brightest than any amount of candles.

"Aunt Marilyn!" Kelly teased. "Remember I have never believed in none of that magic or wishes. I just do what needs doing. And tonight I am going to <u>do</u> my party quick before the lights go out again."

Copyright © American Book Company

Verbs

A **verb** is a word or group of words which is a part of every complete sentence. A verb can describe action which the subject takes or receives. A verb can also link the subject to another word which describes it. Verbs must agree with the subject of a sentence in number and person, and verbs change tense to indicate the time of action.

Consider how you use verbs in sentences and in essays. Generally speaking, a verb tense should not change within an essay without a good, logical reason, but verbs do shift in number with the subject of the sentence. Think for a moment of how you use verbs, and then complete the following exercise.

PRACTICE 8: VERBS

Read the following passage, first for content. Next, proofread for errors in verb form. Neatly strike through the errors, and then clearly write the correct verb above each error. *Hint:* **There are sixteen (16) errors in the text.**

Big Top Follies

Were you going to the movies soon? There is a great film in town. It's been playing at the Dollar Theater, and I saw it last night. The movie are all about a circus clown and his wild ambitions. The clown goes around trying to win weird bets. For example, he betted the elephant trainer this: he could feed an elephant a wrist watch and then find the watch in the elephants' straw, still working. He lose that bet since the animal steps on the watch before the clown can save it. The clown is tried other schemes: he sang for the flamingos, he swim in the crocodile pool, he left flowers for the bearded lady, and he tried to teach the donkey to bow. These bets do not works out. The poor clown then go to the ring-leader of the circus. The clown asking him to think of a bet that he, the clown, can win. The ringleader cannot help but laugh. He do come up with a bet, though. He dares the clown to run for president. He sound serious, but it's a joke. The clown, however, agrees to it. Would you believed this silliness unless you saw it? The clown actually wins the election by a few votes, and he prevented a hand recount. I won't give the end away, but the movie is fueled by mix-ups and Jim Carey-type humor. I was laughing about it right now. I thought about seeing it again, but the real election has been coming soon. I can just watch that.

Copyright © American Book Company

PRACTICE 9: FORMS OF VERBS

Carefully read the passage on this page. Decide how each *boldfaced* verb should be changed, and then rewrite the words on the blanks provided.

Riding Part 2: Mounting a Horse for the First Time

Some horses are elegant and mild creatures; however, some **were**[1] rough and ill-tempered. This last type of horse is an accident waiting to happen. **Did**[2] not let the accident happen to you. There are many ways to protect yourself while enjoying the ride. The first and best protection is education. A professional trainer **can taught**[3] you how to ride. Horses are intelligent, but that does not mean you **should have relied**[4] on their good sense. This basic horse care book **helped**[5] you stay in control. Riding is, above all, a lesson in the age-old communication between humans and horses. People **have rode**[6] horses successfully, for eons.

Mounting: Begin your approach to the horse slowly and quietly. **Spoke**[7] to the horse calmly as you are mounting, and always mount from the left side of the horse. Assuming that the horse is tacked up and held, first **have looped**[8] the reins in the palm of your left hand, and also hold the horn of the saddle with the fingers of your left hand. Second, lift your left foot and slide it through the stirrup; you **are needing**[9] to use your right hand to hold the stirrup steady. Next, reach with your right hand for the back rim (cantle) of the saddle while pushing off with your right foot. Continue that movement, and **swung**[10] your right leg over the saddle. You **are sat**[11] in the middle of the saddle. Be sure to put your right foot into the right stirrup, and **taken**[12] better hold of the reins with both hands. Take a look around before directing the horse to move.

1. _____

2. _____

3. _____

4. _____

5. _____

6. _____

7. _____

8. _____

9. _____

10. _____

11. _____

12. _____

Lie and Lay / Sit and Set

There are two sets of commonly confused irregular verbs. First, there is **lie** and **lay**. Lie is defined as "to recline," while lay is defined as "to place something." They are close in meaning, and in the past tense, lie is spelled lay. The other irregular verbs are **sit** and **set**, which have a similar problem: they are very close in meanings and spellings. See how these irregular verbs are used in the following sentences.

Marian said, "I am going to **<u>lay</u>** my book on the bed before I **<u>lie</u>** down."

Raul **<u>sat</u>** in the café chair and **<u>set</u>** his cup on the table.

Copyright © American Book Company

When proofreading for errors using the verbs lie/lay and sit/set, the first step is to remember that they exist. Also, study the chart below which shows how these verbs are used in different tenses. If you are not clear about the appropriate use of these and other irregular verbs, refer to the companion text, American Book Company's *Basics Made Easy: Grammar and Usage* for lists of these verbs and for practice exercises in using them.

Infinitive	Present Participle	Past	Past Participle
lie (to recline)	(is) lying	lay	(have) lain
lay (to put)	(is) laying	laid	(have) laid
sit (to rest)	(is) sitting	sat	(have) sat
set (to put)	(is) setting	set	(have) set

PRACTICE 10 : LIE AND LAY / SIT AND SET

Read the historical account below, first for content. Then, (circle) the verb from each pair which is correct for the meaning of the sentence. There are eighteen (18) choices to be made.

Casualty of War

During World War I, the United States army kept many of its new recruits in training by (sitting / setting) up temporary camps in rural areas. One such area used by troops was the land (lying / laying) near Black Jack Mountain in Marietta, Georgia. Here, in the early 1900s, one could have seen soldiers (sitting / setting) on pine logs in between training sessions. Part of their training sessions involved learning how to fire weapons, including small cannons, which (set / sat) mini-bombs down upon faraway targets off the side of the mountain. These soldiers never guessed that in the future these pieces of ammunition would be found (lying / laying) on the ground, some still undetonated, and all kinds of people would collect them.

One of the more famous instances of this sort, at least in local lore, was that of a small boy whose father (set / sat) him up into a tree. Using a burlap sack, this father was harvesting pecans, which (lay / lie) under trees in the shadow of Black Jack Mountain. The child (sitting / setting) in the tree saw a hand-sized cannon shell which had (lain / laid) in that tree for decades. The child broke off a limb and tried to pry the shell away from the tree. The father heard his small son's voice calling, "Look what I found!" The next sound he heard was an explosion which echoed off the rocks (set / sit) into the side of Black Jack Mountain.

Struggling back to his feet after having been (laid / lain) flat by the shock wave and the shock, the child's father saw pieces of shattered pecan limbs (lying / laying) over blasted clods of red clay. They say that the man first emptied the sack of pecans, placing them back where they had (lain / laid) before he came, and then he gathered up his child, wrapping him in the rough burlap material to carry him home.

The family and the community (laid / lain) the child to rest in a cemetery near Scufflegrit Road, the turn-off to visit Black Jack Mountain. No memorial was (sit / set) near the place where this young war casualty fell; no Teddy bears nor flowers ever marked the spot. The legend lives on, though, (sat / set) forever into the hearts and minds of a generation of Georgians who grew up (setting / sitting) on front porches listening to the call of whippoor-wills and to the

Copyright © American Book Company

Subject-Verb Agreement

Subject-verb agreement means that both the subject and the verb of a sentence or clause must be of the same number and person. For example, a singular subject must be paired with a singular verb, and a noun in the first person must be paired with a verb in the first person. Consider first how you use verbs to agree with subjects, and then complete the following exercise.

PRACTICE 11: SUBJECT-VERB AGREEMENT

Read the passage below, first for content. Then, proofread for subject-verb agreement. When the subject and verb which do not agree, neatly strike through the error, and clearly write the correct form above each part. *Hint*: **There are fifteen (15) errors to be found.**

Bin There?

Have you ever felt that life was stacked against you? Has you sensed that there is a burden present that presses down unrelentingly? I am experiencing that right now. It are a massive, quivering stack, consisting of squished wood fibers in rectangular shapes, menacingly growing before my face.

Yes! The "To-Be-Recyled" paper collect on my desk, daring me to dislodge it with an ill-advised move. It silently dare me to reach for paper clips or a white flag of surrender. I, now, refers to the stack as the "Re-sigh-call" for help-heap. The really bad news are that no one listens to my pathetic wails drifting through the wall of paper. Neither the management nor the office staff comes to my aid at all.

Instead, the people in my office has impeccable timing. They senses just when the stack has eroded to a manageable level. Then, they marches by with all the righteous solemnity and shallow grief of failed game show contestants, piling their orphaned projects and rejected manuscripts onto my convenient desk. There go another group now. As I fix a withering glare upon the back of the offenders (who can't be bothered to take the stuff out to the bin), the slow march continue until fading into a conference room for the finger-pointing postmortem.

After wishing, vainly, that they suffer some sort of disabling paper-cut on those pointing fingers, I calls for pizza. Moments later, I watches, with a smirk that would leave the Grinch green-er with envy, as the previously preoccupied staff scurry about. Working feverishly, they all carts away enough paper, outside to the recycling bin, so to allow pizza boxes to be centrally deposited. After the meal, who will recycle the boxes?

Yeah, I've "bin" there–head-first in the recycling bin. . . .

 Copyright © American Book Company

Subject-Verb Agreement With Collective Nouns

Collective nouns name single units made up of multiple members. Collective nouns have special rules regarding agreement with verbs. If the unit is truly acting as one as in "A <u>swarm of bees</u> **lives** here," then the verb reflects the singular subject. However, if the unit's members act individually as in "A <u>swarm of bees</u> **perform** their various jobs," then the verb reflects the plural nature of the subject.

Proofreading for collective noun errors concerns the verb form used with them. Think about the logic of using the singular and plural form with the action that is occurring: is it a group or individual action? Then, complete the following exercise.

PRACTICE 12 : SUBJECT-VERB AGREEMENT WITH COLLECTIVE NOUNS

Read the passage below, noting the use of different collective nouns. Then go back, and decide if each collective noun is acting as a group or as individuals. (Circle) one verb in each pair to agree with the subject.

In Pursuit of Trivia

My senior class (know / knows) one thing for sure: we all love trivia. We are putting on plays showcasing our knowledge of it as well as the talents of other students.

The audience (clap / claps) when we act out animal behaviors using obscure collective nouns for groups of animals. For example, when in danger, a knot of toads (leap / leaps) into mud together; when there is a regrettable road kill incident, a murder of crows (take / takes) their favorite positions in the pecking order; and lastly, in a jungle river scene, a crash of rhinos (attack / attacks) a fishing canoe.

It is after this that the other student groups take their turns. First, the band (begin / begins) to play a thunderous medley of hits. Then, the skate club (demonstrate / demonstrates) their different special techniques, with trivial variations in moves. That is a very popular part of the show. Next, the debate team (argue / argues) about the relevancy of trivia. Lastly, the school choir (sing / sings) their favorite, though unheard-of, show tunes.

I believe all this trivia mania began when the student body (was / were) challenged to discover the origin of the school's name: Eagle Lake High School. Well, it was difficult, but our class found the secret. Apparently, the school board (has / have) some members who are avid fans of Andy Griffith: the Mayberry sheriff, you know. So they chose the name to honor him; in the '70s, he starred in a television show, "Adams of Eagle Lake." It ran for only eight days before being canceled. Now that's trivia!

> *Proofread your essay for proper usage of nouns, pronouns, articles, adjectives, adverbs, negative words, and verbs, as well as subject-verb agreement.*

Copyright © American Book Company

SPELLING

Spelling is the process of arranging letters to form words. This may seem simple, but spelling English words can be difficult. The English language has a history of taking words from other languages and trying to make the spelling of them fit into the rules of Standard American English. These rules are rather inconsistent in the first place, so it makes spelling twice as difficult. This chapter will provide you with hints and practice in finding **homonyms** and **incorrect spellings** while you proofread.

Homonyms

Homonyms are words that sound the same, even though they have different spellings and meanings. The best way to proofread for errors in the use of homonyms is to recognize the homonyms that you tend to misuse and look for those first. You may also want to find a list of the most commonly misused homonyms. Study the list so you can recognize common errors.

ant

aunt

PRACTICE 13: HOMONYMS

Read the following essay for content and word meaning. (It continues on to the next page.) Then, (circle) which homonym in each pair is correct for the meaning of the sentence.

Hurdles

Having a birthday can be just (plane / plain) dangerous. You don't believe me? Well, then I'd like to (advise / advice) you better because you haven't had a birthday like mine. It's like this: I had the brilliant idea to take some of my friends to the "Extreme Bike Course" for my 15th birthday. Questioning the safety of this plan, my parents all but said no. They tried to give me wise (council / counsel) and good (advise / advice) instead. However, with serious vows of allegiance to safety gear and pledges of future chores to be done, I (won / one) the day and got the go-ahead.

My friends and I were hyped up for (too / two) weeks while planning this party. We could hardly (bear , bare) the wait. (Whose / Who's) to say that we should have been worried? My parents called the course to check out (it's / its) rules and party arrangements. Finally, the day came, and my dad took us to (were / where) the course was located, out on the coastal (plain / plane). I thought that we would just jump on our bikes and go. Not. (Writing / Righting) the check was the first hurdle that slowed us down, but Dad cleared that (won / one) just fine, filling in the dollar and (sense / cents) in the right places. Dad later described the next paper he had to sign as "(personnel / personal) information. You know, like the instructions on where to send your dead and broken body." He always exaggerates. It was just the usual disclaimer to relieve the bike course (personnel / personal) of any legal responsibility should I become, like, really hurt. I blew this off by showing Dad my safety gear and got my friends to do the same; we were

Copyright © American Book Company

carrying full-body protection to (were / wear). Out-maneuvered, Dad signed the release papers with his eyes shut. What a kidder! Well, after (hour / our) wait, you can imagine how bad we wanted to start. This was taking (two / too) long.

So we took off for the course looking cool in our backwards caps, bike shorts, and shirts with the arms cut out. Well, we wanted our biceps to be (bare / bear) didn't we? As the five of us mounted our bikes, we saw girls in the stands watching for guys; I mean they were trying to act smooth, but we could tell that we were having an (affect / effect) on them, and they were interested.

Interested! Really, they were fascinated, telling us later at the hospital, (were / where) they had followed us, that they had never seen the human body contorted in quite those positions while hurtling through the air like (plains / planes). I won't detail every crash, but you know, it <u>looks</u> easy to do those aerial moves that you see on TV. Lloyd lost a tooth–in his lip; Renaldo ripped his racing shirt and his wrist; Tito twisted and tore all the tendons in his knees; Cal careened into a corner and was concussed; and I, I got injured just where I deserved it, (write / right) in the mouth. I needed stitches inside my cheeks and in my gums: 15 of them in three places each, or 45 to be exact.

That night, using a straw, I celebrated with mashed-up birthday cake and the taste of blood. Dad said it all when he observed that actually wearing the safety gear would have made more (cents / sense). If I make it to my next birthday, he suggested that we rent an Extreme sports video. I was deeply (affected / effected) by his concern, but because of my swollen mouth I could not speak. So, I had to (right / write) my answer–"Yeah, I'm on that."

Incorrect Spellings

Incorrect spellings of words can make your writing sloppy, confusing, or even incomprehensible. Proper spelling is an essential part of effective writing. Because so many words in English have irregular spellings, it is important to memorize commonly misspelled words. It is also helpful to follow a plan when proofreading for spelling errors.

First, consider the spelling errors that are typical for you, and look for those types of errors. **Second**, think about the basic structure of forming words and correct any words that do not follow the structure. **Last**, use your sight memory–the memory which tells you when something just does not look right–and correct the word so it looks right. Using this plan, your proofreading for spelling should be successful.

Before you begin the practice on the following page, think about your own spelling patterns, and think about the rules for spelling that you know. In a notebook, make a list of words that you frequently misspell. Write them ten times each for practice. Be ready to use the proofreading plan (in the second paragraph above) for your spelling errors.

Copyright © American Book Company

PRACTICE 14: SPELLING

Read the following short essay carefully for meaning first. Then, proofread it for spelling errors. When you find a misspelled word, strike through it neatly, and then above the word, write the correct spelling clearly. *Hint:* There are 42 spelling errors in the essay.

NPR TODAY

Are you tring to find an intelligent, meaningful communications source? The easyest way to find what you are seaking is to swictch your radio dial to an NPR station. The National Public Radio station is a frist class educational resource, hepling schools in your city. The public radio stations rely on listeners, ordinery peple, for funding their bugdets. Becuase of that, thy can refuse to run commercials or to counsider big buisness interests befor their audiances' interests.

In this way, public stations can offer viry differrant types of programming and can schedule the programming to meet their listeners' needs. Adults and children can unnite to support this resourse. There are shows which they can enjoiy together or individualy. The public stations, you may kow them as NPR stations, broadcast an interesting vareity of shows about sience, history, cultural movements (includeing sports results), business trends, and film. This is just a bare sampeling of the varied broadcasts ofered to the public by the public (radio). The many station managers and jornalists, your freinds in radio, also foremat their news programs to reelly explain issues and to take time over important events, instead of feeding their listeners sound bites from sleesy politicions' speaches.

Have you found a radio station that could offer all of this? WABE, the public station in Atlana, for example, is one of the best. In Febuarary, this station will be having a fund drive for new fans to jion public radio memebership, allowing them to take control of their destinys. Tune your radio in tommorow to your local public radio station and dicsover, all over agin, how good radio can be.

> *Spelling English words can be difficult, but studying regular and irregular words will bring you success.*

Copyright © American Book Company

SENTENCE FORMATION

Sentence formation is part of the Conventions domain that the GHSWT will evaluate. To demonstrate skill in this area, you must use **end punctuation** appropriately, correct any **sentence fragments** or **run-ons**, correctly identify and punctuate **phrases** and **clauses**, and avoid **misplaced** and **dangling modifiers**.

End Punctuation

End punctuation is one constant in the English language. There are three ways to end a complete sentence.

A period ends a complete statement.

A question mark ends any question.

An exclamation point ends a forceful or emotional statement.

These marks signal a definite end to one sentence and the beginning of the next sentence. End punctuation adds to the organization, variety, and tone of your writing.

PRACTICE 15: END PUNCTUATION

Read the following story carefully, and then add end punctuation as needed. (Circle) each added punctuation. *Hint:* **There are twenty-six (26) end punctuation marks to add.**

GREEN!

Has anyone out there noticed a government plot being carried out in dim grocery store aisles Yes, it's a top secret federal government plot that only certain foreign governments have paid to learn How do *I* know I read Stephen King novels, don't I But you, you need to look around you Look for GREEN; it's leaping out, screaming, grabbing at you everywhere you go

At one time, in years past, parents urged their children to eat green vegetables We are talking about naturally green things And just as naturally, the children turned away, loudly exclaiming, "Yuck " These children are now the grownups driving SUVs Further study reveals an even deeper shame; these are the people who are voluntarily drinking–hold on– be prepared to be sickened They are drinking GREEN TEA Not only is this tea green, but it is flavored with other healthy things: peach, kumquat, lemon, and ginseng What's next, spinach-flavored green tea

Just to make sure that today's kids, those vital elements of target audiences, are not left out, the food industry has now funded research producing a truly grotesque, unnatural form of vegetable–GREEN KETCHUP The marketers using this research are based in Roswell, New Mexico They claim that kid experts chose this color over blue, yellow, and rainbow

But why toy with the artificially-enhanced natural red dye color at all Because, as I said before, it is a government plot They are breaking down taboos–the natural order of the universe It is a law of nature, which Mrs. Einstein recorded: kids <u>hate</u> green food But if the government can break this taboo, breaching the limits of food color, think of all the other ways "Big Brother" can mold us Just watch for the acceptance of green eggs and ham Oh, no What am I saying It's too late

Sentence Fragments or Run-Ons

End punctuation errors may result in **sentence fragments** or **run-ons**. A **sentence fragment** is a phrase that is punctuated like a sentence, but it lacks a subject or a verb. To correct these, simply add the missing element. A **run-on** is the combination of two or more independent clauses with no end punctuation nor internal punctuation. The combining of independent clauses requires either end punctuation or internal punctuation, such as a semi-colon, or a comma with a coordinating conjunction.

You have practiced using internal and end punctuation. Now, you can use commas with the following coordinating conjunctions to correct sentence fragments or run-ons: **for, and, nor, but, or, yet, so**. Remember these words by taking the first letter of each, spelling "**fanboys**."

When writing for a test, you may stop a sentence too soon, or make one sentence blend into the next. As you proofread, make sure each sentence is complete and correctly punctuated.

PRACTICE 16 : SENTENCE FRAGMENTS OR RUN-ONS

Read the passage below. There are both run-ons and fragments in the story. Decide how to best correct each sentence error, and write your answer on the lines that follow. If there is no error, write the word "correct" on the line. Answers may vary.

1 Betsy was not the most graceful or athletic person in our class.

2 Seemed a little klutzy and a natural-born bookworm.

3 In our 7th grade year, however, a vast change.

4 Before, the basketball coach let everyone play he decided to hold team tryouts this year.

5 Appeared to be a challenge to Betsy.

6 She had never been interested in sports now Betsy stayed in the gym after school for weeks before the tryout.

7 Practiced dribbling, passing, and shooting the ball.

8 In classes, bringing books on basketball strategy.

9 Her hard work and single-mindedness got Betsy on the first-string as a guard.

10 We elected Betsy to be the captain of the team she inspired us, on the court and off, in all our years in school.

1 _____

2 _____

3 _____

4 _____

5 _____

6 _____

7 _____

8 _____

9 _____

10 _____

Copyright © American Book Company

Phrases and Clauses

Phrases and **clauses** are two groups of words that help form the structure of sentences. A **phrase** is a group of words that acts as a single unit in a sentence, but it lacks either a subject or a predicate or both. Phrases can function as nouns, verbs, adjectives, or adverbs. A **clause** is a group of words which includes a subject and predicate. There are two kinds of clauses: dependent and independent.

An **independent clause** can stand alone as a sentence. If another independent clause is linked to it, the two clauses must be joined by a comma and a coordinating conjunction (FANBOYS). A **dependent clause** relies on the controlling independent clause in a sentence. The independent clause and the dependent clause are linked together by a relative pronoun such as **which**, **that**, **whose**, or **those**, or by a subordinating conjunction like **while**, **because**, **since**, or **after**.

Being able to recognize these different sentence elements is the first step in learning how to use them in your own writing. You may want to review phrases and clauses in American Book Company's *Basics Made Easy: Grammar and Usage* before beginning this practice.

PRACTICE 17: PHRASES AND CLAUSES

Read the following passage. In the numbered blanks on the next page, write whether the bolded group of words is a dependent clause, an independent clause, or a phrase. (For extra credit identify type of phrase: prepositional, appositive, or participial.)

Team Spirit

All sports teams have similar ways **of celebrating exciting victories** [1]. Even swim teams have big celebrations **after they swim for six hours or longer in meets** [2]. Popular expressions of group joy, **such as head butting and team "dances** [3]," however, are not seen beside the pool. Instead, **there is cheering, eating, dunking, and body art** [4] on display.

    The display of body art is actually created [5] with permanent markers. Coaches write a swimmer's schedule of events on the swimmer's wrist **with the markers** [6]. During the closing two hours of the meet, **the swimmers make their own statements** [7] on their bare skin, usually their arms, and then their legs, and then their backs. (They need help with that part.) The body art at the beginning of a meet is kept to a minimum **because it shows the swimmer's race list and a "Go 'team.'"** [8] But when a team begins to win, the body art becomes more rowdy and silly. The teams try to outdo each other by inventing funny sayings **that won't get them thrown out of the pool area by the coaches** [9].

    Although the coaches stay busy watching for any problems [10], they manage to lead the cheering and celebrating. Parents, grandparents, and other team members cheer especially loudly **when their loved ones are in the water** [11]. Coaches often order fresh pizza to celebrate **before the last race has been swum** [12].

    They do this **when their teams are winning by a gazzilion points** [13]. There is one other big difference between swim teams and other types of sports teams **which involves the party**

1.	_____	8.	_____
2.	_____	9.	_____
3.	_____	10.	_____
4.	_____	11.	_____
5.	_____	12.	_____
6.	_____	13.	_____
7.	_____	14.	_____

Misplaced and Dangling Modifiers

A **modifier** is a phrase or clause that helps clarify the meaning of another word by describing it in more detail. However, if a modifier is positioned incorrectly in a sentence, it can confuse and frustrate the reader.

A **misplaced modifier** is positioned in the sentence too far from what it is modifying. This confuses the meaning, as in the following example.

Example 1: *The painting had visible brush strokes that I was selling.*

In Example 1, it is unclear whether the dependent clause, "that I was selling," describes the painting or the brush strokes. The clause "that I was selling" is a misplaced modifier. To correct this problem, place the modifying clause closer to the word that it describes, as in Example 2.

Example 2: *The painting that I was selling had visible brush strokes.*

A **dangling modifier** is a phrase or clause that comes at the beginning of a sentence but does not modify (describe) the subject in the sentence, as in Example 3.

Example 3: *Dangling from a hook, our bird dove for the worm.*

Does this sentence make sense to you? What is dangling: is it the bird or the worm? Obviously, the worm would be dangling from the hook, not the bird. "Dangling from a hook" is a dangling modifier because its position in the sentence makes it look like it is describing the Subject, "our bird." However, it should be describing "the worm." Correctly wording this sentence would mean changing the position of the modifier, so it is closer to the object it is describing, the worm. Notice this correction in Example 4.

Example 4: *Our bird dove for the worm dangling from a hook.*

Your writing must be clear and logical. Using modifiers incorrectly will confuse your readers. Consider how to make your writing easily understood while using modifiers that add detail and color to your writing. Then, make sure you carefully proofread your sentences for the position of modifiers.

Copyright © American Book Company

PRACTICE 18: MISPLACED AND DANGLING MODIFIERS

Read the following short passage carefully. Then, on the lined spaces below, rewrite the passage, correcting the modifiers that are misplaced or that are dangling.

Family Time?

1   We often lose track of each other being such a large family on trips.
2   So I knew what would happen before we went to the craft show.
3   That's right; we lost someone after we arrived.
4   The booths had a maze of walls where we were looking.
5   Our parents forgot to meet us for lunch running to see everything.
6   Those of us who met for lunch ate hotdogs after looking and calling for them.
7   After taking a boat ride across the lake, too late, our parents remembered the missed lunch.
8   They ate stale chips and a pickle standing up.
9   Sitting together on the fountain, we found them feeding some ducks.
10   We suggested a new plan for our next trip, which will be flawless.
11   Tuning us out, our parents formed their own plans for a no-kids-allowed date.
12   Yelling loud approval, our fists pumped up and down, while insisting that we should have a kids-only party with our friends at the same time.
13   So far, our plans have been left dangling; our hopes have been misplaced: family time rules.

1 _____

2 _____

3 _____

4 _____

5 _____

6 _____

7 _____

8 _____

9 _____

10 _____

11 _____

12 _____

13 _____

> *To demonstrate skill in sentence formation, you must use end punctuation appropriately, correct any sentence fragments or run-ons, correctly identify and punctuate phrases and clauses, and avoid misplaced and dangling modifiers.*

CHAPTER 6 SUMMARY: PROOFREADING THE ESSAY

- *Standard proofreading notation is not necessary for the Georgia High School Writing Test, but make your corrections neatly and clearly, so that the graders can easily read your essay.*

- *Certain words are capitalized to emphasize their importance. These words include the first word in a sentence, proper nouns, words in titles, etc.*

- *Use the appropriate internal punctuation within your sentences, including commas, colons, semi-colons, apostrophes, and quotation marks.*

- *Proofread your essay for proper usage of nouns, pronouns, articles, adjectives, adverbs, negative words, and verbs, as well as subject-verb agreement.*

- *Spelling English words can be difficult, but studying regular and irregular words will bring you success.*

- *To demonstrate skill in sentence formation, you must use end punctuation appropriately, correct any sentence fragments or run-ons, correctly identify and punctuate phrases and clauses, and avoid misplaced and dangling modifiers.*

Copyright © American Book Company

CHAPTER 6 REVIEW: PROOFREADING THE ESSAY

A. **This exercise will help you with the proofreading plan that you have learned and practiced in the chapter. Read the essay first for content. Then, read with an eye for internal punctuation, correct grammar usage, spelling, and sentence formation.**

When you find an error, use the proofreading marks which you have seen in the chapter. You may refer to page 123 if you wish. Neatly strike through the error, and clearly write the correct form above the error. If there are any problems with the content, note that separately at the end of the essay.

Writing Situation

   A local bridal and tuxedo shop is offering a lifetime coupon for a free wedding to the winner of their latest contest. The participants in the contest must write an essay describing the best place to get married. People used to get married only in religious buildings or court houses, but today, people get married in places such as on an airplane, on the beach, or even under the water. What do you think is the best place to get married?

Directions for Writing

   Write an essay in which you persuade the contest judges of the best place to get married. Use specific details and clear reasoning to support your choice.

Odd Places To Get Married

Traditionaly churchs and chapels were the main places for young couples to get wed. In the past twenty years or so people have gone away from the traditional wedding's. To be married where you have meet is not that unusual or bizarre. Many couples have been getting more adventureous in their wedding locations; couples marry where they are happiest too. All of these choices are just that: choices. Weddings need to be meaningfull to the people involved. Four popular places where they get married are underwater, on the beach, on a airplane, and sometimes in their schools.

Getting married underwater involves many factors and variables. First, a scuba-diver lisence needs to be obtained for the bride and groom. So the new couple will need a blood test, and also a swimming test. Second, a good scuba-diving location needs to be found, for example, Key West and the red sea and the Barrier reef is considered the best diving spots in the world. Third, a pastor or priest with scuba-diving experience need to be found. Those could be a difficult search. Underwater weddings cost the mostest money because of the extra variables. But if that kind of wedding is meaningful to the new couple, I'd say that they should go for it.

Getting married on the beach is a odd but romantic place to take wedding vows Standing in the sand with the waves roaring, and the sun setting can be romantic. Except for the danger of a jellyfish or stingray alert. Starting the honeymoon after a sting from one of those sea cretures could be unpleasant even with a romantic full moon and the smell of suntan oil. One advantage of beach weddings is that the wedding and honeymoon can be in the same city. Virgin Islands, Cayman Islands and Jamaica are good examples of places people pick for their meaningful, for them beach weddings.

Airplane weddings have become a odd place for people too get married. Airplane weddings are small due to space. Some people like to parachute out of the plane after taking their wedding vows. Airplane weddings can be very expensive and difficult to plan. Because of having to rent a plane and the skydiving equipment and having to have good whether. There would also need to be a separate place for the the reception or party afterwards. The things that must be considered are: food (airplane food?), flowers (thrown to the winds?), and which hospital is closest (in case the wedding is no longer the main event 'cus of injury). But flying free while being married can be very meaningfull to some couples.

This last example of an odd wedding makes a school wedding seem very respectable. To be married where you have met is very romantic and sweet. If two people can learn to love each other they also need to learn how to live together as a married couple what better place symbolizes that intention than a school. Even if space may be cramped in the hallway, there is always a gym or cafeteria for lying out food and presents. Also most of the guests would be old friends and very familiar with the location; so no maps needed to be printed. All these people could help decorate with posters and streamers, and help mix the party punch. This is a win-win situation. The school is appreciated for it's community service, the new couple has a cheap but happy memory.

Getting married should be fun and a unforgettable memory. Underwater weddings and airplane weddings are more costly than beach and school weddings. People for some time have been looking for odd; yet meaningfull places to get married. The most popular odd places to take wedding vows have been underwater on the beach on airplanes, and in a place of youth, memory and magic; the old school house. Support the two people who want to get married at our school. The media attention will benefit the school and our place in the community. So write letters and call talk shows for the sake of true love and for fame.

Copyright © American Book Company

B.   For the Review in Chapter 5: Revising the Essay, you revised several different essays which you wrote for the Chapter 4 Review. Return to those essays now. Proofread them based on the skills that you have practiced in this chapter. You may want to use the checklist below to help you.

☐   I made my corrections neatly and clearly.

☐   I checked for errors in capitalization.

☐   I corrected errors in internal punctuation including, commas, colons, semi-colons, apostrophes, and quotation marks.

☐   I corrected any errors in grammar and usage, including nouns, pronouns, adjectives, adverbs, negative words, verbs, and subject-verb agreement.

☐   I made sure all words are spelled correctly.

☐   I looked for errors in sentence formation, including end punctuation, fragments, run-ons, and misplaced modifiers.

C.   In Chapter 5, Practice 7: Revising (page 116), you revised several different essays. Based on what you have learned about proofreading, return to these essays and correct any errors you find. Use the checklist above to help you.

ADDITIONAL ACTIVITIES: PROOFREADING THE ESSAY

1. Select 3-4 essays from your portfolio. Practice proofreading these essays. Based on what you learned in this chapter, correct any errors.

2. Choose one essay from your portfolio, and exchange it with another student. Proofread each other's essay. Explain the errors you find in each other's essay. Then, make the corrections, and rewrite your essays.

3. After you make your corrections and rewrite your essay, give it to your instructor to look for any errors you may have missed. Make special note of the errors you overlooked, so you don't overlook them on the Georgia High School Writing Test.

4. Read several articles in your local newspaper. Look for proofreading errors that the newspaper editors may have missed. Even professional writers make mistakes!

5. With one other student, choose two Web sites from the list in Appendix B. You and your partner will each visit one of the Web sites. Find instruction and activities that will help you with proofreading. Report back to your partner, and compare the strengths and weaknesses of each Web site.

6. Look over all the essays in your portfolio, and make a list of your most common errors. Practice the skills you need to overcome these errors. On the Georgia High School Writing Test, make sure you proofread first for these most common errors.

7. From all of the essays in your portfolio and the practice exercises in this book, make a list of the words that you have difficulty spelling. Share your list with the class, and make one big list of commonly misspelled words. Study these words in preparation for a spelling bee. Also, write a persuasive essay to convince your instructor what prize the winner should receive. Then have a spelling bee in which the winner gets a prize.

Copyright © American Book Company

Chapter 7
Scoring the Essay

Since you are a student writing the essay, not a professional reader grading the essay, why should you practice scoring essays? There are two reasons: it will help you become a better writer, and it will help you perform better on the Georgia High School Writing Test (GHSWT).

An important part of the writing process is reviewing. A good writer steps back from his or her work, takes time away, and returns to the work with a fresh outlook. Then, the writer can see more clearly which ideas are unrelated and which need more development. Errors in grammar and punctuation stand out more, and the writer can hear whether the tone is appropriate and consistent throughout the essay.

Scoring your own work or the work of student peers is excellent practice for reviewing. To determine a score for an essay, you must distance yourself from the work and use an objective scale to evaluate the work. This process will help you develop better skills in reviewing your own written works, thus making you a better writer.

As you score your own paper and the papers of your student peers, you will be using the criteria (or standards) for the GHSWT. In this process, you will become more familiar with the writing skills that the professional graders will evaluate. Then, you will be more able to include those skills in your own writing, so you can write a better essay for the Georgia High School Writing Test.

This chapter provides you with a scoring overview, as well as detailed scoring information about the four domains. The domains provide the guidelines for scoring the Writing Test. They include the following areas:

- **Ideas**
- **Organization**
- **Style**
- **Conventions**

This chapter also contains some sample essays for you to practice scoring. The best practice, however, is for you, your peers, or your teacher to review your essays and work together to score them.

SCORING OVERVIEW

As the graders read your essay for the GHSWT, they will be looking for several general requirements. The graders will also evaluate specific writing skills in four domains, or areas of writing. The graders will use a five-point scale in their holistic grading of your essay. Holistic grading means that the graders will look at the essay as a whole, taking both strengths and weaknesses into account, and not simply count the number of errors.

Copyright © American Book Company

Requirements

To make sure your paper can be graded properly, you must do the following:

Write on the assigned topic. Make sure you clearly understand the topic, purpose, and audience for your assignment. Keep a clear focus, and do not stray from it.

Write in English. This test is intended to evaluate your skill in writing Standard American English.

Write legibly. You want the graders to be able to read your essay easily. You may have great ideas, but if the graders can't read them, you will not get credit for them.

Write a well-developed composition. Though you have only 100 minutes, this is enough time for you to organize your ideas into a three- to five-paragraph essay. Write an introduction, one to three paragraphs of support, and a conclusion.

Write in prose. This is not a test in poetry. Extended use of musical lyrics will not be graded.

Write respectfully. Essays that use offensive language or discuss offensive content may not be graded. If you can't express your ideas without vulgarity, then don't express them.

Write on the two pages of lined paper. Your final draft must fit on the two pages provided for the test. The graders will not consider any writing outside this space, including your prewriting.

Write your own essay. You may not copy a published source or another student's writing.

By fulfilling these requirements, you guarantee only that your paper will be graded. For your paper to receive a passing grade or an excellent grade, you must demonstrate skill in the four domains (or areas of writing skill) outlined in the next section.

Domains

As you read in the introduction to the Diagnostic Writing Test at the beginning of this book, the graders will score your essay according to the following four domains and their components. Notice that the first domain counts twice as much as the other three.

1. **Ideas (40%)** The writer establishes the controlling idea through examples, illustrations, facts, or details that are appropriate to the persuasive genre. This domain includes the following components:

   - Controlling idea/focus
   - Supporting ideas
   - Relevance of detail
   - Depth of development
   - Awareness of the persuasive purpose
   - Sense of completeness

Copyright © American Book Company

2. **Organization (20%)** The degree to which the writer's ideas are arranged in a clear order and the overall structure of the response is consistent with the persuasive genre. This domain includes the following components:

- Overall plan
- Introduction/body/conclusion
- Sequence of ideas
- Transitions
- Grouping ideas within paragraphs
- Organizing strategies appropriate to persuasion

3. **Style (20%)** The degree to which the writer demonstrates control of sentence formation, usage, and mechanics. Note: In general, sentence formation and usage are weighted more heavily than mechanics in determining the overall conventions score. This domain includes the following components:

- Word choice
- Audience awareness
- Voice
- Sentence variety

4. **Conventions (20%)** The writer forms sentences correctly. This domain includes the following elements:

- Sentence formation: correctness, clarity of meaning, complexity, end punctuation
- Usage: subject-verb agreement, standard word forms, verb tenses
- Mechanics: internal punctuation, spelling, paragraph breaks, capitalization

Five-Point Scale

Graders use a five-point scale like the one below to determine the score for each domain. The scale shows the amount of control of the components of a domain within the essay.

Little or No Control	Minimal Control	Sufficient Control	Consistent Control	Full Command
1	2	3	4	5

One paper may be a "high 3" and another may be a "low 3," but both papers receive the same score. In judging between scores, it may help to think that if the paper is more like a 4 than a 3 and more like a 4 than a 5, then 4 is the appropriate score.

Analytic and Holistic Grading

The scoring system is analytic, which means that more than one feature of your essay is evaluated. How well you do in each domain counts together to make up your final score. Each domain itself is scored holistically, which means that the domain score comes from each test rater's overall impression of how well you understand and use the features of a domain.

As you practice scoring, consider how well each essay meets the criteria in each domain. For example, when looking at the domain of **Conventions**, a short essay may be free of grammatical errors, but it may be too short to cover the topic well. On the other hand, a longer essay may have a number of errors, but overall, the paper may show that the writer truly understands the topic and the mode of writing. This would be an example of a good score in the **Ideas** domain outweighing a lower score in **Conventions**.

Copyright © American Book Company

Georgia High School Writing Test: Scoring Rubric

Domain 1: IDEAS. The degree to which the writer establishes a controlling idea and elaborates the main points with examples, illustrations, facts, or details that are appropriate to the persuasive genre.

Components

- Controlling Idea/Focus
- Supporting Ideas
- Relevance of Detail
- Depth of Development
- Awareness of the Persuasive Purpose
- Sense of Completeness

To achieve a score of 5: Full command of the components of Ideas. The writing is characterized by most or all of the following:
- Fully focused on the assigned topic and persuasive purpose
- Fully developed controlling idea that establishes the validity of the writer's position
- Supporting ideas and elaboration are relevant to the writer's argument and audience
- Supporting ideas are fully elaborated throughout the paper with logical examples, details, and evidence (facts, expert opinions, quotations, or commonly accepted beliefs)
- Uses rhetorical devices to support assertions (e.g., appeal to emotion, anecdote, analogy, logical reasoning)
- Response contains an abundance of information that fully addresses readers' concerns, counterarguments, biases, or expectations

To achieve a score of 4: Consistent control of the components of Ideas. The writing is characterized by most or all of the following:
- Consistently focused on the assigned topic and persuasive purpose
- Well developed controlling idea that establishes the validity of the writer's position
- Supporting ideas and elaboration are relevant to the writer's argument
- Supporting ideas are consistently well developed with specific examples, details, and evidence
- Uses some rhetorical devices to support assertions (e.g., appeal to emotion, personal anecdote, analogy, logical reasoning)
- Response contains complete information and addresses readers' concerns, counterarguments, biases, or expectations

To achieve a score of 3: Sufficient control of the components of Ideas. The writing is characterized by most or all of the following:
- Sufficiently focused on the assigned topic and persuasive purpose
- Sufficiently developed controlling idea that establishes the writer's position
- Most supporting ideas are relevant to the writer's argument
- Supporting ideas are developed with some examples, details, and/or evidence
- Some parts of the paper may be well developed, but other parts of the paper are only partially developed
- Response is generally appropriate to the persuasive purpose and may include some rhetorical devices
- Response contains sufficient information to provide a sense of completeness and address some reader concerns

To achieve a score of 2: Minimal control of the components of Ideas. The writing is characterized by most or all of the following:
- Minimally focused on the assigned topic and persuasive purpose
- Minimally developed controlling idea that addresses some aspect of the writer's position
- Some points and details may be irrelevant or inappropriate to the writer's argument
- Supporting ideas are vague, general, and/or undeveloped
- Some ideas may be partially developed, while others are simply listed without development
- Response demonstrates minimal awareness of the persuasive purpose
- Response lacks sufficient information (due to incomplete development or the repetition of supporting ideas) to provide a sense of completeness and address reader concerns

To achieve a score of 1: Little or no control of the components of Ideas. The writing is characterized by most or all of the following:
- Little or no focus on the assigned topic and/or persuasive purpose
- Writer's position may be apparent, but a controlling idea is not established
- Ideas do not advance the writer's position
- Ideas are unclear, irrelevant, and/or repeated
- Response does not demonstrate awareness of the persuasive purpose
- Lacks a sense of completeness and fails to address reader concerns
- Insufficient student writing (due to brevity or copying the prompt) to determine competence in Ideas

156

Copyright © American Book Company

After studying the rubric on the previous page, read the tips below on scoring the Ideas domain, and score the essays that follow.

Scoring Ideas

Clear Controlling Idea/Focus: Your paper must be clearly organized around a **controlling idea** that addresses the assigned topic and has a persuasive purpose. The controlling idea is a brief summary of your focus and establishes your position for the essay. Though the controlling idea may be implied, stating the idea directly is helpful to the reader. A direct statement of the controlling idea can also help you maintain your focus while you write.

Supporting Ideas, Relevance of Detail, and Depth of Development: Use facts and appeals to emotion to support your controlling idea. This support may include assumptions, reasoning, emotion, irony, humor, examples, testimony, or data. Make sure that your **supporting ideas are related to your argument** and that they are **fully elaborated** with appropriate examples and details. Because the test does not allow time for research, you will not be graded on whether these ideas are factually correct or incorrect. However, they should make sense and sound reasonable.

Awareness of the Persuasive Purpose: Your writing should be focused on establishing a convincing point of view on a topic. In addition, you should demonstrate an awareness of the persuasive purpose by anticipating reader concerns and addressing different perspectives that are related to your controlling idea.

Sense of Completeness: The reader must have a sense of completeness about the paper as a whole. You must be sure that there are no gaps in the information you present. In addition, the concluding paragraph must lead the grader to a sense of ending and a summary of the whole argument.

Read the essay on the next page, and use the rubric and tips to score the essay in the domain of Ideas. The essay is a response to the writing prompt below. (It is the same prompt used for the Diagnostic Essay at the beginning of this book.)

Writing Situation

In the past, schools hired their own cafeteria staff to provide nutritious, home-cooked student lunches at a low price. Today, private food service companies are claiming that they can provide better school lunches at lower prices. Your local school board is considering a proposal which would allow several food service companies to set up operation in the school cafeteria. Some parents are concerned that students will eat nothing but "fast food." Decide what you think about private companies providing school lunches.

Directions for Writing

Write a letter to the school board that clearly expresses your position on private companies providing school lunches. Try to convince the board members to agree with you by using well-developed arguments.

To whom it may concern:

I thiink the school Board should let private comanies come into the cafeteria and sell their food. It would be a good opportunity since they could sell their food to us. The food in the cafeteria right now is bad so it would be better to have someone else come in and do it. Here are some reasons why.

When the lunch bell rings at school, most kids groan because they have to go to the cafeteria and find some to eat. The food doesn't taste good and it even smells bad. How would you like to face that everyday at lunch? I wouldn't.

Another reason why the food is bad in the cafeteria is because they serve the same thing every couple weeks. The cooks in the cafeteriea are probably board because they cook the same thing nearly every week. The students are board. Because they have to eat the same thing almost every week. Some people say you can bring your own lunch. What kind of lunch can you bring that you can leave in your locker? Nothing that sits in the locker all morning is going to taste any good by lunch time. So, private companies would make this sitution better.

Private companies can bring in a lot of different food because they don't cook the same thing all the time. They make food that tastes good because they won't sell any if its not good. They would make the food in the cafeteria much better. And maybe the students would stop complaining then. Even the teachers don't like the food.

So as you can see, the school borad should let private companies come into the cafeteria and sell us food. It would taste better than the food that is there now and kids would be happier. They would probably do better in school, too. And that's a good thing. Even if you wouldn't expect it from just getting better lunches. I hope you make the right decision.

Sincerly, Sharon McPherson

How did you score this essay? It may look well thought out, but it really isn't. The controlling idea is clear: the food in the cafeteria is bad, and private companies would make it better. Also, the essay follows the five paragraph structure and even has connecting phrases like "Here are some reasons why." The ideas are not well developed, however, mostly because the writer provides very little support for her controlling idea. While she states that the food in the cafeteria is bad and that private companies would make it better, she does not support this position with specific examples. In fact, the fourth paragraph is a series of circular arguments. The writer also introduces seemingly related information that does not support her arguments, such as that cafeteria workers are bored and that teachers don't like the food. The conclusion introduces the idea of improved student performance due to better lunches. The conclusion is not the place to introduce a new idea. Because this essay is flawed in the domain of Ideas, it would probably receive a score of "2." Go back to the rubric, and try revising this essay.

PRACTICE 1: SCORING IDEAS

Read the following essay, and assign it a score for Ideas. On a separate sheet of paper, explain why you gave the score. For extra practice, on your own or in a group, revise and improve the essay for a higher score.

Essay 1 responds to the writing prompt on page 157 about allowing private companies to provide lunches in the school cafeteria.

Copyright © American Book Company

1.   School lunches have never been a favorite of mine. I prefer to bring my lunch to school. That way I have control over what goes into my food. Some people think I'm kind of a health nut, but it's not like I grow my own food or just eat nuts and berries all day long. I just think it's important to put good food in your body, and that's why I don't think private companies are the answer to the school lunch question.

The last thing a I want to do when I walk into the cafeteria is see all the flashing lights and "on sale today" signs that will inevitably result form unrestrainted capitalistic competition in the cafeteriea. I want to eat in peace. I guess the cafeteriea is not the best place for that. That's why I sit outside on days with good weather.

The school cafeteriea staff tries to keep things a little interesting. Think about the nice holiday meals at thanksgiving and Christmas. And they cook the food on a three week rotating schedule of menus. Some students think that's too repetitive, but hey, if you think about it, you don't even get that much varieaty at home. Kids think if their not eating at home, then thier eating out and they should have menu selections like thay do at McDonald's or Pizza Hut. Who would want to go there on a regular basis anyway?

The staff in the school cafeteria work hard to provide decent meals. They don't do that great a job, but they try real hard. The only way these private companies could get us food at a lower cost is to mass produce some meal, ship it hear and then throw it in the microwave to get it hot. They can't bring thier whole kitchen to the school and cook just for a fraction of the student body. The cafeteria workers buy in bulk and cook the food here. That's the cheapest way to do it.

So I'd have to say that it's better not to let the private companies come in. They will just bombard us with their ads, give us fast food on a regular basis, and serve reheated specials day after day. The school cafeteria gives us reasonably healthy food with reasonable variety, at reasonable prices. What more could you ask for?

Essay 2 is a response to the following prompt. Read the essay, and give it a score based on the rubric and tips for the domain of Ideas.

Writing Situation

There is growing concern regarding the need for better lighting around your school. There are many, though, who consider the lighting adequate. The school board has asked the PTA to help. Before the PTA decides whether to raise the funds, it wants to gather opinions from parents, teachers, and students regarding the need for new lights. What do you think about the lighting around your school?

Directions for Writing

Write a letter to the PTA expressing your opinion about the need for new lights around your school. Try to convince the PTA to agree with your position by using well-developed supporting arguments.

2.   "It is better to light one candle than to curse the darkness." With the growing crime rate in the neighborhoods around our school, many members of our school are becoming fearful and angry. They want to spend a significant amount of money on increased lighting around the school. It seems to me that we can sit around discussing the issue as the darkness closes in, or we can light a few halogen candles to scare the darkness away.

Some people say that new lights are a waste because students go to school during the day. "What good are big lights in the day time?" they say. Well, these people have not taken the time to notice the dwindling daylight hours of winter. As winter approaches, many students who have special activities before school, arrive in the dark. Others students who are involved in the various after-school extracurricular activities offered by our fine school do not leave the campus until after the sun has gone down. These students need to feel safe as they are traveling to and from school. New lighting around the school would accomplish this worthy goal.

Opponents of the new lights obviously do not take advantage of the various entertainment opportunities offered by our school. The winter season is filled with performances by our choir and our band. The talented actors at our school perform their plays at the end of the first semester. Not to mention the athletes who play on our basketball, track, and swim teams. The growing darkness around our school could scare away the people who usually come to these events for personal enjoyment. Often, these people contribute to the good for the school through donations of time and money. It is well worth the investment in new lighting to keep these fine people coming to the special events at our school.

Finally, the new lights at the school will save money from being spent on clean up and repair from vandalism. Thank God that our school has been spared from all but a few minor cases of vandalism. But the circle of graffiti and broken windows continue to shrink tighter around our school. Police bulletins advise that sufficient lighting is the best deterrent to vandalism around your home. The same is true of our school.

The cost of lighting is significant. However, when the benefits of the lights are compared to the costs of darkness, it is clear that "it is better to light one candle than to curse the darkness." I hope and pray that the members of the PTA will "see the light."

ORGANIZATION

The Organization domain refers to how you put your ideas together. Can the reader easily follow your ideas, and are they presented in a logical order? Does your essay flow smoothly from paragraph to paragraph? This domain consists of the following components:

Scoring Organization

Overall Plan and Introduction/Body/Conclusion: Before you start writing your draft, make sure you know where your essay is headed; otherwise, you may find yourself with an introduction that states one idea and a conclusion that addresses something different (or even contradictory)! You can avoid this problem by thinking of your overall plan in the prewriting or brainstorming stage. Also, ease your reader into the essay with a brief but engaging introduction that clearly states your position. Save your supporting evidence and details for the body paragraphs, and sum up your ideas in the concluding paragraph. In maintaining closure, you should also try to leave an impression in your readers' mind, convincing them that your argument is sound.

Sequence of Ideas and Grouping of Ideas within Paragraphs: Ideas should progress in a logical order so that the reader can follow your argument, and related ideas should be grouped together within paragraphs. Do not introduce many different ideas in one paragraph; it is better to discuss few ideas thoroughly than many ideas superficially.

Organizing Strategies Appropriate to Persuasion: Your paper should follow a definite **pattern of organization** that is effective for a persuasive purpose. There are many ways to arrange the ideas in an essay. Chapter 1 of this book discussed four methods, including spatial order, time order, order of importance, and contrasting ideas. There is no single way to organize ideas in your essay, but the order you choose should be clear to the reader.

(Continued)

Transitions: Your paper should have a variety of smooth transitions both between paragraphs and within paragraphs. If the grader doesn't know how you got from one idea to another, you are missing a transition. You want to lead the reader through the essay with **one idea flowing to the next**. Use the transitional words and phrases you studied in Chapter 4 to receive full credit on this aspect of your essay.

Georgia High School Writing Test: Scoring Rubric

Domain 2: ORGANIZATION. The degree to which the writer's ideas are arranged in a clear order and the overall structure of the response is consistent with the persuasive genre.

Components

- Overall Plan
- Introduction/Body/Conclusion
- Sequence of Ideas
- Grouping of Ideas within Paragraphs
- Organizing Strategies Appropriate to Persuasion
- Transitions

To achieve a score of 5: Full command of the components of Organization. The writing is characterized by most or all of the following:
- Organizing strategy is appropriate to the writer's argument. The overall strategy facilitates the writer's communication of ideas
- Logical and appropriate sequencing of ideas within paragraphs and across parts of the paper
- Introduction engages the reader and sets the stage for the writer's topic and persuasive purpose
- Conclusion provides a sense of closure without repetition
- Related ideas are grouped in a logical manner within paragraphs
- Uses effective and varied transitional elements to link all elements of the response: parts of the paper, ideas, paragraphs, and sentences. Transitioning extends beyond the use of transitional words and phrases

To achieve a score of 4: Consistent control of the components of Organization. The writing is characterized by most or all of the following:
- Overall organizing or structure is appropriate to the writer's argument and topic. Structure guides the reader through the text
- Appropriate sequencing of ideas (e.g., order of importance, cause and effect, advantages & disadvantages)
- Introduction sets the stage for the writer's topic and persuasive purpose
- Conclusion provides closure without repetition
- Related ideas are grouped together in paragraphs
- Varied transitional elements link parts of the paper and link ideas within paragraphs

To achieve a score of 3: Sufficient control of the components of Organization. The writing is characterized by most or all of the following:
- Organizing strategy is generally appropriate to the writer's argument and topic
- Clear sequence of ideas
- Conclusion provides closure
- Introduction fits the writer's topic and/or persuasive purpose
- Majority of related ideas are grouped together in paragraphs
- Transitions link parts of the paper or ideas within paragraphs

To achieve a score of 2: Minimal control of the components of Organization. The writing is characterized by most or all of the following:
- Organizing strategy is formulaic and/or inappropriate to the persuasive purpose
- Minimal evidence of sequencing
- May lack an introduction or include an ineffective introduction
- Conclusion may be lacking or limited to the repetition of the writer's position and supporting ideas
- Some related ideas are grouped together in paragraphs
- Minimal use of transitions (transitions may be formulaic, ineffective, or repetitive)

To achieve a score of 1: Little or no control of the components of Organization. The writing is characterized by most or all of the following:
- Little or no evidence of an organizing strategy
- Lacks an introduction and/or conclusion
- Lacks transitions or uses inappropriate transitions
- Ideas are not sequenced in a meaningful order
- Unrelated ideas are included within paragraphs
- Insufficient writing (due to brevity or copying the prompt) to determine competence in Organization

PRACTICE 2: SCORING ORGANIZATION

Read the following essays, and assign each a score for Organization. On a separate sheet of paper, explain why you gave these scores. Then, revise the essays for higher scores.

Essays 3 and 4 respond to the writing prompt below.

Writing Situation

The school counselor has been visiting your English class to offer help in choosing a career. The members of your class are indecisive regarding their careers. The counselor has suggested going to either extreme. He wants students to write an essay about either why they would really want a particular job or why they would really not want a particular job. Think about what career you would really like or not like.

Directions for Writing

Write an essay describing a career you would really want or one that you would really not want. Use clear examples and solid reasons to support your choice.

---

3.   This is quite an unusual topic. I've never been asked what I <u>don't</u> want to be. I <u>don't</u> want a job pushing papers. I like to work with my hands, and to be free to move about. I can't be locked into some desk job, scribbling and typing my life away. I don't want any job where I am required to look busy or business-like, or make idle chatter by the water cooler or coffee machine. Barely can I stand the choking stench of an "office" (A.K.A. Claustrophobic Nightmare). A place of physical and mental decay, where drones trade their souls for a pension and a paycheck. Not me, dear heart, not I. I must be where clouds roam like buffaloes of yore and sunlight, like a tidal wave, drenches and covers all that it can. I do not a stagnant job in a stagnant city. Driving my stagnant car and living my stagnant life. To that I kindly reply "No, Thank You. I'll just sit over here in the corner and paint something . . ."

4.   President of the United States used to be the sole dream of my early childhood. Having been born outside of the United States on a U.S. Naval Base, I was concerned about whether or not I would be permitted to run for the candidacy. After learning that I would be able to run for office, but discovering what politics was all about, my dream was shattered.

        Looking back on the idea of being President of the United States now, appears to me to be ridiculous. Without the power of the Senate behind the President, the office is empty and useless. If the President were to be given more power in the voting process I would reconsider my opinion. All decisions that come out of Washington D. C. now, are nothing more than a shakedown between the Republicans and the Democrats. Besides, the President will always have to worry about pain and death, not only to himself, but to all of the American people as well.

        One quote from William Shakespeare would be a great description of childhood, "Ignorance is bliss". In childhood one does not have to worry about whether or not his dream is plausible or what all that dream would include. Overall, I have decided that the office of President of the United States will be better suited to someone who enjoys the game of politics, and not by myself who would actually like to enjoy life without the pressure of relection.

Copyright © American Book Company

STYLE

Style is a certain way of expressing thoughts or feelings. People often speak of a "style of dress" or a "style of house." For example, the same actress is pictured to the right in two very different styles. Style also refers to the way a writer expresses ideas or emotions. For the Georgia High School Writing Test, the domain of Style includes the following components:

Score the next essays based on the tips below and the rubric for the Style domain on the next page.

Scoring Style

Word Choice: Your word choice needs to be appropriate for your audience, topic, and tone. You also want to use specific words. For example, you should replace a general word like talk with more specific words such as whisper, shout, blab, or babble. Each of these words describes a particular manner of talking. In addition, be sure you use appropriate adjectives and adverbs to accentuate your argument. Effective word choice is discussed in Chapter 4 of this book on pages 77-81.

Audience Awareness: The writing prompt will indicate that you should address a particular audience. It may be other students, parents, a legislator or some other person(s). Each audience is concerned with certain issues. The support for your position should take that into account. Also, your word choice and tone should be appropriate for the specified audience. For example, if you are writing to the zoning board to approve an under 21 club in your city, you should point out the club's benefits regarding keeping teens out of trouble and not focus just on entertainment. You should also use a respectful and formal tone.

Voice: In the same way that we all have different voices when we speak, we also have our own "voices" when we write. The words you use when you write communicate certain aspects of your personality to the reader. Your voice, also known as tone, is the attitude you express toward the topic and the audience. Make sure the voice you use in your paper is appropriate for your audience and purpose. Different examples of voice include sarcastic, humorous, candid, ironic, respectful, etc. Keep your voice consistent so the reader will not be confused about your meaning or intent.

Sentence Variety: A series of similar sentences may be clear and correct but lacking in style. Each sentence in an essay is connected to those around it. By varying the structure of your sentences, you create interest and emphasize certain points. Return to pages 114-115 in Chapter 5 for a discussion of sentence variety.

Georgia High School Writing Test: Scoring Rubric

Domain 3: STYLE. The degree to which the writer controls language to engage the reader.

Components

- Word Choice
- Audience Awareness
- Voice
- Sentence Variety

To achieve a score of 5: Full command of the components of Style. The writing is characterized by most or all of the following:
- Carefully crafted phrases and sentences create a sustained tone and advance the writer's purpose with respect to the intended audience
- Varied, precise, and engaging language that is appropriate to the persuasive purpose
- Word choice reflects an understanding of the denotative and connotative meaning of language
- Figurative or technical language may be used for rhetorical effect
- Sustained awareness of audience throughout the paper
- Evocative or authoritative voice that is sustained throughout the response
- An extensive variety of sentence lengths, structures, and beginnings

To achieve a score of 4: Consistent control of the components of Style. The writing is characterized by most or all of the following:
- Language and tone enhance the persuasive purpose
- Word choice is precise and engaging
- Awareness of audience in the introduction, body, and conclusion
- Consistent and distinctive voice
- Sentences vary in length and structure

To achieve a score of 3: Sufficient control of the components of Style. The writing is characterized by most or all of the following:
- Language and tone are appropriate to the persuasive purpose
- Word choice is generally interesting and appropriate with occasional lapses into simple and ordinary language
- Awareness of audience in the majority of the paper (some parts may lack audience awareness)
- Writer's voice is clear and appropriate
- Some variation in sentence length and structure

To achieve a score of 2: Minimal control of the components of Style. The writing is characterized by most or all of the following:
- Language and tone are uneven
- Word choice is simple, ordinary and/or repetitive
- Minimal awareness of audience
- Minimal, inconsistent, or indistinct voice
- Minimal variation in sentence length and structure

To achieve a score of 1: Little or no control of the components of Style. The writing is characterized by most or all of the following:
- Language and tone are flat and/or inappropriate to the task and audience
- Word choice is incorrect, imprecise, and/or confusing
- Little or no awareness of audience
- Writer's voice is not apparent or controlled
- Little or no sentence variety
- Insufficient student writing (due to brevity or copying the prompt) to determine competence in Style

PRACTICE 3: SCORING STYLE

Essay 5 responds to the writing prompt below. Read the essay, and score for Style. Then also read essay 6, and give it a score for Style. On a separate sheet of paper, explain why you gave the essays those scores. For extra practice, on your own or in a group, revise and improve the essays.

Writing Situation

    Once again, the controversy over prayer in schools is being discussed at your school. Some say that prayer is beneficial for students and teachers. Others claim that it forces religious beliefs on students. Decide how you feel about prayer in schools.

Directions for Writing

    Write a letter to the editor of your local newspaper describing your position on prayer in schools. Describe the reasons for your position, and try to convince others to agree with you.

---

5.   Here we go again! Prayer in public schools. Prayer in public schools. Prayer in public schools. How many times to we need to revisit this issue? The principle in the Constitution of the United States is clear: separation of church and state. Trying to enforce prayer in school is like trying to tell people what favorite color they should have. Who would decide what color should be your favorite? How would they enforce it? And what happened to my right to have my own opinion? These are the same questions I ask about the subject of prayer in public schools.

    Don't get me wrong. Just because I don't think there should be prayer in public schools doesn't mean I don't think people should pray. I have Christian friends, Jewish friends, Muslim friends, and the list goes on. I've gone to pray with them at their places of worship and found the experience truly enriching. That doesn't mean that I'm going to join their religion. It just means that I respect their beliefs and I can see why it works for them. I would not, however, want them telling me that I have to pray like them, which is what the school would be doing if it mandated school prayer. The school board, or someone else, would have to ask, "Which prayer? Muslim, Christian, Jew, Hindu? Would it rotate on a weekly basis? What about non-mainstream religions?" You can see the difficulty here.

    The next major problem with prayer in schools is how to enforce it. Let's say we did have a time of prayer in the morning. What if I chose not to say the prayer? Would the teacher give me a detention if she didn't see my lips moving at the right time. Would I get a bad grade in prayer? Would I not graduate? Even if we had a time of silence, the same problem would arise. What are we supposed to do during that time of silence? And how wold a teacher know what was going on in my head or in my heart?

    Lastly, I support the idea that we all have the right to believe what we want, and that we have the responsibility to learn about different ways of thinking. So, I propose that we have a religion class in school. Just teach the history and beliefs of the various mainstream religions. Each of them has had a significant impact on the history of the world. They also play an important role in the current political affairs

Copyright © American Book Company

around the globe. Along with the history and beliefs, students could study and experience different prayer forms by going on field trips to different places of worship. This educational experience would broaden students' minds and give them a greater appreciation for the wonderful diversity within the human family. That is what public school education should be about.

Let's put an end to this debate about prayer in public schools. They say that "As long as there are tests, there will be prayer in schools." This may be true, but the students do it how they want and when they want. Prayer in public schools is difficult to regulate and impossible to evaluate. A better educational approach would be to require a comparative religions course that teaches understanding and appreciation for various forms of religious expression.

Essay 6 responds to the following writing prompt.

<u>Writing Situation</u>

It's the end of the year, and your parents are cleaning out the closets to make a donation to a local charity. They want you to evaluate your collection of clothing and decide what you want to keep and what you want to give away. They think it will be helpful for you to decide which is your favorite article of clothing and write a letter to them describing why.

<u>Directions for Writing</u>

Write an essay entitled, "My Favorite Piece of Clothing." Include strong support for your choice, so that you may win the contest.

6.   Dear Mom and Dad,

I know you probably think that the dress you bought me for Christmas last year is my favorite article of clothing. I really do love that dress and I appreciate you giving it to me. But I would have to say my favorite article of clothing is my concert t-shirt from the Christina Aguilera concert I went to. As you know, I wear this shirt all of the time. Primarily, I wear this shirt because it takes me back to her concert.

There we were-a bunch of screaming fans when she came on stage. She started singing immediately when the lights came on. I would have to say that her voice is one of the best I have ever heard, her voice sounded strong, assertive, and positive. These are all qualities I admire and try to imitate. I really liked to listen to her lyrics describing love and relationships. Being through many relationships myself. I could definitely identify with some of the situations she describes in her songs.

When she sang, I sang along with her. I had memorized every word from her latest CD. She sang with such feeling that I felt she really had gone through many of the things she sings about. I felt that her singing was genuinely from her heart. Which is more than I can say about most bands these days.

To summarize, every time I wear my Christina Aguilera shirt, I feel that I am reliving the concert and experience. In some way, I guess, I am hoping that her performing qualities, her strength, assertiveness, genuineness, and positive attitude, will some how rub off on me. So you see, Mom and Dad, I have good reasons that I like this T-shirt the best of all my clothes.

Sincerely,
Priscilla

Copyright © American Book Company

CONVENTIONS

Conventions are general agreements about basic principles. For example, there are certain conventions about how to address a letter so that the post office will mail it to the right person. If you don't follow the conventions, the letter doesn't get to the place you want it to go. In the same way, if you don't follow the conventions of written language, your ideas will not get to the reader in the way you want. There are rules that authors, teachers, and all writers agree to follow. These rules define **Standard American English**. Even if it's not the way you speak or write in casual situations, these are the rules you must learn to ensure that others will understand what you write in more formal or academic contexts. The graders for the GHSWT will be looking for the following components in the Conventions domain:

Scoring Conventions

Sentence Formation: Sentence formation refers to how you organize your words into complete sentences. A sentence is like a train: it needs a beginning, a middle, and an end. If any part is missing, you don't have a complete sentence. The parts also need to be connected properly, or they will come apart. A sentence without end punctuation is like a train without a caboose. You don't know where one sentence (or train) ends and another begins. Clauses within a sentence that are not connected with the appropriate conjunctions are like train cars that come apart as the train winds around a curve. A properly connected, complete train stays together. In order to achieve **clarity** in your writing, make sure your sentences do the same. Also, be sure that your sentences have the appropriate level of **complexity:** avoid writing too many short, choppy sentences.

Usage refers to how you "use" the English language. The graders will score your essay based upon the rules and practices of Standard American English. The graders will be looking for clear and correct pronoun references, proper verb tenses, correct agreement of subjects and verbs, and the appropriate form of adjectives and adverbs. Slang and jargon are inappropriate for the Writing Test and will reduce your score unless they are used in a quote from someone. You are also expected to use English words appropriately, including commonly confused words such as accept/except, to/two/too, sit/set, and lie/lay. (See American Book Company's *Basics Made Easy: Grammar and Usage Review* for a more in-depth study of usage.)

Mechanics includes capitalization, punctuation, spelling, and format, according to the rules of Standard American English. Errors in both end punctuation and internal punctuation are considered in the domain of Conventions. Errors in mechanics are distinguished from oversights in **proofreading**.

Format refers to the appearance of your paper and includes standard writing practices of margins, paragraph indentation, spacing between words, and spacing between sentences. The graders will consider these aspects of your paper, but they will not evaluate the conventions specific to letters, even if the prompt requires a letter.

Proofreading is the writer's final review of a piece of writing. In this stage of the writing process, the writer looks to correct errors in capitalization, punctuation, spelling, and grammar. A flaw in proofreading, such as the repeated word in "I am going to go go to the store," does not indicate an error in mechanics. Such a flaw does not count as much as an actual error in mechanics, such as the missing helping verb and article in "I going to go to store."

Based on the descriptions of the components of the Conventions of Written Language domain, you should score papers according to the following scale.

Georgia High School Writing Test: Scoring Rubric

Domain 4: CONVENTIONS. The degree to which the writer demonstrates control of sentence formation, usage, and mechanics. *Note: In general, sentence formation and usage are weighted more heavily than mechanics in determining the overall conventions score.*

Components:

Sentence Formation	Usage	Mechanics
• correctness	• subject-verb agreement	• internal punctuation
• clarity of meaning	• standard word forms	• spelling
• complexity	• verb tenses	• paragraph breaks
• end punctuation		• capitalization

To achieve a score of 5: Full command of the components of Conventions. The writing is characterized by most or all of the following:
• Full command of simple, complex, compound, and complex/compound sentences with correct end punctuation
• Consistent clarity of meaning even in complex sentences
• May include functional fragments
• Variety of subordination and coordination strategies
• All elements of usage are consistently correct: subject-verb agreement, word forms (nouns, adjectives, adverbs), verb tense, pronoun-antecedent agreement
• All elements of mechanics are consistently correct: punctuation within sentences, spelling, capitalization, and paragraph indentation
• Infrequent, if any, errors

To achieve a score of 4: Consistent control of the components of Conventions. The writing is characterized by most or all of the following:
• Consistently correct simple, complex, and compound sentences with correct end punctuation
• Consistent clarity of meaning at the sentence level
• May include functional fragments
• Most elements of usage are consistently correct
• Most elements of mechanics are consistently correct
• Errors are generally minor and do not interfere with meaning

To achieve a score of 3: Sufficient control of the components of Conventions *or two components may be strong while the other one is weak.* **The writing is characterized by most or all of the following:**
• Majority of sentences are formed correctly with some complex and/or compound sentences, but there may be some fragments and run-ons
• Sentence level meaning is generally clear
• Usage is generally correct, but there may be some errors in each element
• Mechanics is generally correct, but there may be some errors in each element
• Few errors interfere with meaning

To achieve a score of 2: Minimal control of the components of Conventions *or one component may be strong while the other two are weak.* **The writing is characterized by most or all of the following:**
• Simple sentences may be formed correctly, but there are frequent fragments and/or run-ons
• Some end punctuation may be incorrect or lacking
• Mixture of correct and incorrect instances of the elements of usage
• Mixture of correct and incorrect instances of the elements of mechanics
• Some errors may interfere with meaning

To achieve a score of 1: Little or no control of the components of Conventions. The writing is characterized by most or all of the following:
• Frequent sentence fragments, run-ons, and unclear sentences
• End punctuation is incorrect or lacking
• May contain frequent and severe errors in most elements of usage
• May contain frequent and severe errors in most elements of mechanics
• Errors may interfere with or obscure meaning
• Insufficient student writing (due to brevity or copying the prompt) to determine competence in Conventions

Copyright © American Book Company

PRACTICE 4: SCORING CONVENTIONS

Read the following essays, and assign each one a score for Conventions. On your own paper, explain why you gave the essay that particular score. For extra practice, on your own or in a group, revise and improve the essays.

Essay 7 is a response to the following prompt:

Writing Situation

> The rising number of accidents involving teen drivers has sparked a debate about raising the age requirement for obtaining a driver's license. Some argue that teens under 18 are too immature to handle the responsibilities of driving. Many teens, however, have come to depend on cars to get them to and from work and school. What do you think about raising the age requirement for obtaining a driver's license?

Directions for Writing

> Write a letter to your state representative expressing your opinion about the age requirement for obtaining a driver's license. Support your opinion with clear reasoning that will convince your audience to agree with you.

7.   Learning to driver is one of peoples main things to learn now. Driving as good and bad pointes. The good thinges are geting from places'es far off to see kin, to work, or even shopping.

         Some people don't understand that drinking and driving killes other people. Druges also as the same effect on killing people. The law now is .1 is drunk driving.

         Learning to drive is every 16 year oldes dream. They can go out on dates, be with friendes, or just go riding around town, or back roades.

         Teen agers are 50% of the drunk drivers. The state law at less to be 18 year or older before geting licesen.

         The reson why it is important to me now is because, it get me home, to see my Kin, help me get my billes paied, and get me to school.

Essay 8 is a response to the following prompt:

Writing Situation

> When the issue of environmental conservation came up in your science class, it caused a heated debate. Some students felt that individual choices don't make a difference because the world is so big and so many governments and companies are polluting. Other students felt that each person's choices contribute to the improvement or decline of the earth's environment. What do you think about the effect you can have on the health of the global environment?

Directions for Writing

> Write an essay in which you describe your feelings about the effects of individual actions on the environment. Use clear examples and convincing arguments to persuade other students to agree with you.

Copyright © American Book Company

8.   Everyone can make a difference. I, also, felt the task of making the environment cleaner and safer was daunting and believed there was nothing I could do. However, that was just an excuse, an easy way out. All things start with one person–you. Others then usually follow the leader, and convince others to go along with the movement, this phenomenon is known as peer pressure.

      Most of the time, peer pressure is discussed as a negative term, with destructive effects. Drug abuse, the growing acceptance of pre-marital sex, alcoholism, and even the growth of gangs and teenage suicides. Peer pressure is a forceful tool, we need to grasp it from those using it to undermine society and use it to the advantage of everyone.

      You, as one member of a global village, can accomplish many things using peer pressure. To begin with, you can recycle your own garbage such as old newspapers, aluminum cans, and broken glass. Next, convince your friends to be part of your effort by telling them of all the advantages, and how they can make a difference.

      There are many problems which come from lack of care for the environment. Someone at a particular point in time must seize the initiative to fix these problems. If you truly believe in the cause, you will do your part. Get started today.

      Sometimes you may get discouraged over the way things are going, or lack of going anywhere. Do not lose heart. Keep in mind, you took the initiative when no one else would. You have planted seeds that change minds in the many people around you. You cannot fail. It is not your task to change the entire world. Even small changes in our own backyards can go a long way.

For additional practice scoring, review each of the 8 student essays in this chapter, and score them for additional domains. For example, review essays 1 and 2, which you scored for the Ideas domain, and score them for Organization, Style, and Conventions. Then, score essays 3 and 4 for Ideas, Style, and Conventions, as so on. Review your scores and comments with your teacher.

This practice will help you to learn the components of each domain even better. In addition, as you score more papers, you will gain further knowledge about what to do and not do when writing your essays.

Copyright © American Book Company

CHAPTER 7 SUMMARY: SCORING THE ESSAY

The Four Domains for the Georgia High School Writing Test

1. **Ideas (40%)** *The writer establishes the controlling idea through examples, illustrations, facts, or details that are appropriate to the persuasive genre. This domain includes the following components:*

   - *Controlling idea/focus*
   - *Supporting ideas*
   - *Relevance of detail*
   - *Depth of development*
   - *Awareness of the persuasive purpose*
   - *Sense of completeness*

2. **Organization (20%)** *The writer's ideas are arranged in a clear order and the structure of the response is appropriate to the persuasive genre. This domain includes the following components:*

   - *Overall plan*
   - *Introduction/body/conclusion*
   - *Sequence of ideas*
   - *Grouping of ideas within paragraphs*
   - *Organizing strategies appropriate to persuasion*
   - *Transitions*

3. **Style (20%)** *The writer uses language that engages the reader. This domain includes the following components:*

   - *Word choice*
   - *Audience awareness*
   - *Voice*
   - *Sentence variety*

4. **Conventions (20%)** *The writer demonstrates control of sentence formation, usage, and mechanics. It is important to note that sentence formation and usage are weighted more heavily than mechanics in determining the overall conventions score. This domain includes the following components:*

   - *Sentence formation (correctness, clarity of meaning, complexity, end punctuation)*
   - *Usage (subject-verb agreement, standard word forms, verb tenses)*
   - *Mechanics (internal punctuation, spelling, paragraph breaks, capitalization)*

The Five-Point Scale

Little or No Control	Minimal Control	Sufficient Control	Consistent Control	Full Command
1	2	3	4	5

Copyright © American Book Company

CHAPTER 7 REVIEW: SCORING THE ESSAY

On your own or in a group, rate each of the following essays on a five-point scale for each aspect of the essay: *Ideas, Organization, Style, and Conventions*. **On separate sheet of paper, give reasons for the score you assigned to these essays. Compare your ratings with those of other students or your instructor.**

<u>Writing Situation</u>

Your parents are concerned about your grade report for this semester. Your grades dropped considerably. They blame your involvement in extracurricular activities and your part-time job. They want you to focus on school and drop all outside commitments. What do you think would be the best solution?

<u>Directions for Writing</u>

Write a letter to your parents and present a solution with which both you and your parents can agree. State your opinion clearly and include reasons and logic that will convince your parents that your solution is the best one.

---

1.   Dear Mom and Dad,

I really am deeply disappointed in myself for the drop in the grades I received this semester. I believe the challenge of adjustment to the new job coupled with my extracurricular activities, made my academics bad. However, I think I can pull up my grades this semester by dropping my extracurricular activities and keeping my part-time job.

The extracurricular activities I was in: the marching band, Interact Club, and Toastmasters International, took up a lot more time than my part-time job. All together, these three activities took up twenty hours of my time per week and I am probably being conservative with that figure. This lack of time directly affected my academic performance because I had less opportunity to do my homework and study for tests.

The job, while challenging at first is now much easier to manage. Working in fast-food was very difficult for me. Now, however, I can do my job easily. The job also takes less time than my extracurricular activities did. I spent a maximum of 18 hours per week working part-time. With the money I earn, I can take on more responsibility by making my car payments, insurance, and fuel charges.

In conclusion, you will watch my grades go up, because I have more time to study and have a feeling of responsibility. Dropping my other activities will free up my time to study and do my homework. Continuing to work helps me retain a sense of adult responsibility and will give me a degree of respect for myself. Please allow me to keep my job, I promise to quit if my grades do not improve during the second semester.

Sincerely,
Lahiri Singh

Copyright © American Book Company

Writing Situation

The recent purchase of two books for the school library has caused controversy among members of the library's advisory panel. Some members of the panel want the books banned from the school, while other members feel that the books are appropriate for high school students. The panel is debating the issue next week and is seeking input from parents, students, and teachers about banning controversial books from the school library. What do you think about banning books from your school?

Directions for Writing

Write a letter to the school library's advisory panel. State your position on banning controversial books from the library. Support your viewpoint with specific reasons and examples. Persuade the panel to agree with you.

2. To the members of the Advisory Panel,

I would like to respond to the question put before this panel concerning the school policy of banning books which some students and parents find objectionable from the school library. Censorship is tool that supposedly protects students from reading morally objectionable material. This tool is not effective for two reasons. First, the banned book gains celebrity and increases its popularity as an alluring "forbidden fruit." Second, students have other ways to gain access to these books. Together, censorship as a policy will have the opposite effect to what it is intended.

Let us first consider the notoriety a book gains once it is banned from schools. The press is eager to pick this as a controversial story. When students and parents sit down and watch the news, they learn of this book. Some parents will purchase it just to see what others find objectionable. In fact, previous sales reports show that controversy surrounding a previously obscure book can elevate it to bestseller status. Many people would go their whole lives without ever picking up this objectionable book. Once the book is publicly scrutinized, however, many people will hurriedly go to the bookstore and purchase it to find out what all the fuss is about.

Secondly, students are crafty. If they really want to go around their parents and purchase this material, they will find a way. If the book is banned from the school libraries, this student may go to the public library and check it out. If the book is banned from all public libraries, the student can earn the money necessary to purchase it from a bookstore. They can take the book home and hide it in a special place where their parents will not find it.

In conclusion, because censorship brings free publicity to a morally objectionable book, and students will not be stopped from getting access, censorship is an ineffective tool. Many parents will be intrigued as to the contents of this book. Students, who do not need objectionable influences in their lives, will now be tempted to purchase a morally depraved book. It is much better for students to make positive choices about the material they read. If the students feel forced to make the right choice, however, the results could backfire.

Sincerely,
Tamara Johnston

Copyright © American Book Company

Writing Situation

A video arcade company has placed a bid on an acre of land next to your high school. The arcade company plans to build a video arcade and a fast food restaurant on the property. School administrators and some members of the community are concerned that this development will negatively affect students in your high school. What do you think about putting a video arcade right next to your school?

Directions for Writing

Write a letter to the principal in which you explain your opinion about building a video arcade and restaurant next to your school. Convince the principal to agree with your opinion. Provide reasons and examples to support your viewpoint.

3. There would be nothing better for this community than to have an arcade come right next to the high school. People here wouldn't worry about where their kids are, because they would be in the arcade. It would be good if the city could pay for the arcade. That way, all of the games can be for free!

The arcade would motivate kids to do better in school. You parents could say, "Now Johnny, if you want to go to the arcade after school I'd better see straight A's on your report card." Now we all now Johnny or Alice will work hard in school so they can spend their leisure time at the arcade after school.

Also, playing video games improves eye-hand coordination. This coordination is an important life skill. Otherwise, you can't do things in life like tie your shoes or catch a ball!

In conclusion, you gotta let kids play or they'll go nuts! Video game depravation could lead to numerous mental disorders such as depression and schizophrenia. School administrators, let the kids play and you will make better and brighter students!

Writing Situation

A local television station has chosen a panel of high school students to debate the following question: "Should students be held back if their grades and test scores show that they are not ready to be promoted to the next grade?" You will serve as a guest on this panel for an upcoming television show called "Teens Today." What is your position on this issue?

Directions for Writing

Write an essay that states your position on this issue. You will refer to this essay during a debate on the television show "Teens Today." Persuade your peers that your position makes the most sense. Include convincing reasons and examples to strengthen your argument.

Copyright © American Book Company

4.   Promoting students even though they are not performing well academically may seem like a good idea, but the results will be increasingly bad for the child. Initially, the self-esteem of the student may be affected. However, with time, the student will benefit from being held back. Learning is a building process. If you don't understand something at one point, you will be unable to understand at later points. Students that have been allowed to go forward end up doing worse the following year in all of these subjects.

Now some teachers and parents may say that the little kid's feelings might get hurt if he or she is held back, but that kid is going to end up in worse shape if you let him or her keep going! You school board members better take a second and smell the coffee! Do you want the kid to do well throughout school. Or do you want the kid to get frustrated later and think about quitting in tenth grade? The choice is yours!

ADDITIONAL ACTIVITIES: SCORING THE ESSAY

1.   The following two essays respond to the question: "What characteristics must a student possess to be successful in college?" Read each essay, and decide which one is more effective. Write an explanation of your decision based on the four domains of *Ideas, Organization, Style, and Conventions*.

A.   When students decide to go to college, they have many responsibilities to obtain their college degree. After they have been accepted into college, they must remember some points on how to be successful. Students could be successful because they have good attendance, and they have good study habits.

First of all, students must have a good attendance record. They have to be in their classes each class period, so that thy would not miss important information. You must maintain passing grades. These grades have to be at least an A, B, or a C to pass any college class. You must attend learning labs. You have to participate in these labs to help you understand your class more better. These labs also help students to comprehend their class information.

Last of all, students must have good study habits. They have to learn to dedicate themselves to their course of study. They must motivate their time. Students have to be involved in their research of their class. They must attend lectures. All of these things help students to complete their course of study. When students have graduated from college, they could give themselves credit for all the hard work. They know how to be successful in college. So what, College was difficult. Students would have learned that college was worthwhile.

B.   Today, with the seemingly infinite numbers of student's attending college, it is important to be successful in order to receive a quality education. In receiving a quality education a student must possess certain characteristics. The characteristics that students must possess are good study habits, good note taking skills, and good listening skills.

Copyright © American Book Company

175

First, students must have good study habits in order to be successful in college. To insure good study habits a student should make a study schedule in order to allow him or her to have time to study everyday. This way students will not have to cram the night before an exam. When a student is studying he or she should be in a studying frame of mind. The student should think about what he or she is doing so that they can get the most out of there time. He or she should try to keep focused and have a good attitude. Also, the students should pick a study place like there room, if it is quiet. If the students room is not quite, then they should pick a place that is. One that has no distractions. Usually the library and lunch room are not good places to study because their are to many distractions. For example, the students eating lunch and the clouds outside. The students can not keep focused therefore they do not learn the material as well.

Second, students should have good note taking skills. The students should review there material before they start so that they can get an idea of what they will be taking notes on. Also students should take notes on what they are studying and what the teacher is going over. When the teacher is lecturing the students should try to abbreviate and not write sentences so that they can get as many notes down as possible. The students can always go back and fill in the sentences later if they like writing in sentences. If the students are still having trouble than they should ask another student if they could look at there notes.

Finally, the students should have good listening skills. If the students do not havegood listening skills than there note taking skill will probably be poor to. The students should try to be attentive and assertive. Also, the students should try not listen to what there classmates are saying next to them and should not talk in class. The students can not learn if they are talking. Another suggestion to help better the students listening skill is for them to eat a good healthy breakfast. This will give the students energy and help them stay awake. The students can not learn if they are asleep.

In conclusion, one can see that there are many important skills and habits a student needs in being successful in college. The students not only needs to be successful, but also be the best. No matter how hard college gets the students should not give up because the reward of a degree will be wonderful.

2. Review 3-4 essays you have written in response to the writing prompts in this book. On a separate sheet of paper, rate each essay according to the four writing domains evaluated by the GHSWT. Provide reasons for your ratings.

3. Exchange your essays from Activity 2 with another student or with members of a small group. Have each student score the essays based on the four writing domains discussed in this chapter. Discuss and compare your ratings for each essay with the ratings from other students. Are your ratings similar or different? Why? Why not?

4. Have your teacher or tutor rate the essays you chose for Activities 2 and 3. How does your teacher's or tutor's ratings compare with yours and those of other students? What might account for the similarities and differences in the ratings?

5. Revise your essays based on the combined feedback you received from your teacher or tutor and your student peers. Submit your essays to your teacher or tutor for a new rating based on your revision. Were the ratings and input from your teacher and other students beneficial? Why? Why not?

Copyright © American Book Company

APPENDIX A: SAMPLE WRITING PROMPTS

1. <u>Writing Situation</u>

The hairstyles, clothing, and jewelry of students in today's schools often reflect current fads and fashions that are sometimes controversial. Are dress codes necessary in today's schools, or should students be allowed to dress as they wish?

<u>Directions for Writing</u>

Write a letter to the principal in which you defend your position for or against dress codes in schools. Use clear reasoning as well as your own experiences and observations to convince the principal to agree with you.

2. <u>Writing Situation</u>

The hairstyles, clothing, and jewelry of students in today's schools often reflect current fads and fashions that are sometimes controversial. Are dress codes necessary in today's schools, or should students be allowed to dress as they wish?

<u>Directions for Writing</u>

Write an editorial for the school newspaper in which you argue for or against dress codes in school. Use well-developed arguments to try to convince other students to agree with you.

3. <u>Writing Situation</u>

Your family is considering getting a new pet. Some members of the family welcome the proposed addition, while others think that the pet will be another nuisance in the house. Your family is considering a dog, a fish, a cat, or a gerbil. To make this decision, your parents have asked each family member to write a letter that makes an argument for or against a specific pet. How do you feel about having a new pet?

<u>Directions for Writing</u>

Consider the positive and negative aspects of having a dog, a fish, a cat, or a gerbil as a pet. Write a letter to your family explaining whether or not to have a pet. Try to convince your family members to agree with you by providing well-developed supporting arguments.

4. Writing Situation

   Recently, a student in New Mexico wanted to wear traditional Native American dress over her cap and gown for her high school graduation. The school district refused to grant her request. Should students be required to wear a cap and gown to participate in graduation ceremonies? Should they be permitted to add other items of clothing to their cap and gown? Think carefully about your position on this issue.

Directions for Writing

   Write a letter to the district school board members in which you clearly assert your position on the cap and gown requirement. Try to convince the board members to agree with you by using well-developed arguments.

5. Writing Situation

   Many professional athletes earn millions of dollars each year while teachers, nurses, firefighters, and law enforcement officers earn much less per year. Is it fair that professional athletes earn such high salaries compared to these public servants? Why? Why not?

Directions for Writing

   Write your opinion to the editor of the local newspaper. Include reasons and evidence that will convince the newspaper subscribers to support your position.

6. Writing Situation

   Your yearbook is going to include an award for a student who is "Most Likely to Succeed." You want to nominate a student for this award. Why do you think this student deserves to win this award? In what ways do you think he or she is likely to succeed?

Directions for Writing

   Write a letter to the school yearbook staff in which you nominate a student for the award of "Most Likely to Succeed." Be sure to include specific examples that support your choice.

7. Writing Situation

   Citizens and conservationists alike are concerned about the poor air quality in many big cities. Cars, buses, planes, and industry contribute to this pollution. You have been asked to speak at a community forum on this issue.

Directions for Writing

   Write a speech that you will give at the community forum. Convince your audience of the best ways to improve air quality in your community.

Copyright © American Book Company

8. Writing Situation

    Some people today live together in extended families where parents, children, grandparents, and other relatives all share the same house. Other people live in nuclear families consisting of only parent(s) and child(ren). Your local library is sponsoring a "Families First Forum." One of the discussions will be about these two different kinds of families. How do you feel about this issue?

Directions for Writing

    Write an essay that you will read at the "Families First Forum" arguing for either nuclear or extended families. Include arguments and evidence that would persuade other families to support your position on this issue.

9. Writing Situation

    Recently two suicides by students have occurred in your school district. The school community is deeply concerned that these tragedies may continue. The guidance counselor has requested that you write an essay for the school newspaper about the issue of suicide.

Directions for Writing

    Write an editorial in your school newspaper persuading the reader that suicide is not a way to solve problems. Include reasons and evidence that will convince your readers to support your position.

10. Writing Situation

    Inventions such as the cell phone, television, cars, iPods, and computers have changed the way people live. Some people feel the changes have been for the better, while others think the changes have been for the worse. If you had the power to eliminate any invention in the world, what would it be?

Directions for Writing

    Write a letter to one of your friends complaining about a particular invention that you do not like. Describe the problems with the invention. Include reasons and evidence that will convince your friend to support your point of view.

11. Writing Situation

    One of your friends is considering going to work on a full-time basis in addition to staying in school. Your friend feels the need to increase her income in order to increase her standard of living. Her parents feel that her grades will suffer if she works full-time, and she may even flunk out of school. You know her well, what do you think?

Directions for Writing

    Write a letter to your friend convincing her to agree with your opinion about working and school. Use clear and convincing reasons that will persuade her.

Copyright © American Book Company

12. Writing Situation

A new way to stop crime is being considered in your area. Under a new law, people who are ticketed for more than three traffic violations would be required to display a sign on the door of their car listing a phone number to the department of public safety. Other drivers could call the number to report any other violations committed by this driver. Is this a fair policy or not?

Directions for Writing

Write an editorial in your local paper discussing your position on this policy issue. Include reasons and evidence that will convince the readers of your paper to support your decision.

13. Writing Situation

Suppose that the current laws in your community permit citizens to cite other residents for disturbing the peace if their dog barks excessively. These citations can lead to fines and court hearings. However, people reporting the disturbance can do so anonymously and do not have to provide proof that the dog has, in fact, barked. Should this law be considered appropriate? If the law is not appropriate, how would you change the law to make it appropriate?

Directions for Writing

Write a speech that you will present before the local animal control board. Be sure to persuade members of the board to agree with you by using well-developed arguments.

14. Writing Situation

One day on your school campus, you see a dog and a police officer who are at the school to check the grounds for the presence of drugs. You talk to people on campus about the presence of the dogs. Some students are thankful that the dogs are there, while other students complain that their privacy is being invaded.

Directions for Writing

Write your school board a letter either supporting or opposing the board's decision to allow police dogs to sniff for drugs. Make your argument clear, complete, and convincing.

15. Writing Situation

One of your relatives tells you that parents are ultimately responsible for their children's success. You think about this statement and form an opinion. Are parents or their children more responsible for school success? Explain your viewpoint clearly.

Directions for Writing

Write a letter to your relative in which you either agree or disagree with him or her. Try to convince your relative that your viewpoint is valid by providing well-developed supporting arguments.

Copyright © American Book Company

16. <u>Writing Situation</u>

You are entering a competition to get an article published in the *New World Journal*. The editors of the magazine are asking potential contestants to write a paper convincing the readers to pick one exercise as the healthiest physical activity for their New Year's resolutions. What physical activity do you think is the healthiest?

<u>Directions for Writing</u>

Write an article to be published in a national periodical. In the article, you promote one physical activity as the best for good health. Provide clear reasons and appropriate examples to support your opinion.

17. <u>Writing Situation</u>

Confucius once said: "Choose a job you love, and you will never have to work a day in your life." However, many people feel that they can't make enough money at the job they would really like to do. As part of an exercise in choosing a career, your guidance counselor wants you to think about what you consider more important in a job: job satisfaction or a high salary. What is your opinion?

<u>Directions for Writing</u>

Write an essay for your guidance counselor about the importance of job satisfaction versus a high salary. Use a clear and reasoned argument to convince the counselor to agree with your position.

18. <u>Writing Situation</u>

Shopping on the Internet increases by 300% each year. Purchasing products is quick, easy, and usually tax-free. Should Internet shoppers be required to pay federal and state taxes like people who shop at malls and stores? Why? Why not?

<u>Directions for Writing</u>

Write an editorial for your local newspaper in which you either support taxation of Internet purchases or oppose it. Make your argument clear, complete, and convincing for subscribers of the paper.

19. <u>Writing Situation</u>

Your social studies class has been discussing marriage. Some people remain single all of their lives, while others get married. Many marriages end in divorce, and then people get remarried. The entire class has been discussing the emotional and practical issues of marriage. Do you think the single life is better than marriage?

<u>Directions for Writing</u>

Your teacher is requiring each student to write an essay regarding marriage, and then read it to the class. Write your essay which advocates either the single life or marriage. Provide solid reasons so that other students will agree with you.

20. <u>Writing Situation</u>

The wonders of modern medicine have made it possible for more people to live longer than ever before. Many consider the added years a blessing that allows people to do more with their lives than they thought possible. Others, however, feel that the poor quality of life that elderly people experience is a curse more than a blessing. How do you feel about people living to be 90 or 100 years old?

<u>Directions for Writing</u>

Write an article for the school newspaper that answers the question, "Do you want to live to be 100?" Provide reasons and well-developed explanations for your answer.

21. <u>Writing Situation</u>

The teacher in your civics and government class asked the students to answer the following question: "Should the personal life of the President of the United States reflect high moral standards, or is the personal life of the President of the United States irrelevant to his/her public contributions?"

<u>Directions for Writing</u>

Write an essay for your civics class in which you present your opinion about how the personal life of the President of the United States relates to his or her job performance. Convince your teacher to agree with you by using well-developed arguments.

22. <u>Writing Situation</u>

Some families and state governments are suing cigarette manufacturers for smoking-related deaths. Several cities are now involved in bringing lawsuits against gun manufacturers for gun-related deaths. Do you think gun manufacturers should be sued for gun-related deaths?

<u>Directions for Writing</u>

Write a letter to your district attorney trying to convince him or her that suing gun manufacturers is or is not a good idea. Make your argument clear, complete, and convincing.

23. <u>Writing Situation</u>

Some students drop out of school before earning a high school diploma. A bill currently before the state senate would bar high school dropouts from driving until they are nineteen years old. Should high school dropouts be denied driver's licenses until they are 19 years old, or should all teenagers of legal age be allowed to drive whether they attend school or not?

<u>Directions for Writing</u>

Write a letter to your representative in the state legislature persuading him or her to your position regarding high school dropouts and driver's licenses. Develop your argument using well-thought-out supporting ideas.

Copyright © American Book Company

24. <u>Writing Situation</u>

One of your friends makes the following comment to you: "It's not <u>what</u> you know that counts, but <u>who</u> you know." Do you think knowledge and skills or social contacts are more important for success?

<u>Directions for Writing</u>

Write a letter to your friend. Explain to him or her whether your agree with the comment or not. Persuade your friend by using well-thought-out and reasoned arguments.

25. <u>Writing Situation</u>

In recent years, pit bulls have injured or killed children and adults in the United States. A citizen action committee is launching a campaign to require all pit bulls to be registered by the county as dangerous animals. The county would also have the power to "put to sleep" any pit bull which bit a human being. Would you support this law? Why or why not?

<u>Directions for Writing</u>

Write an article to be published in your local newspaper. Clearly state your position regarding the treatment of pit bulls. Try to convince the readers of the article to agree with you by providing well-developed supporting arguments.

26. <u>Writing Situation</u>

The impact of video games on culture in the United States has received much attention. The issue has acquired even more importance as a local radio station this week asks listeners to respond to the following question: "Is playing video games harmful or beneficial for human beings?" Decide how you feel about this issue.

<u>Directions for Writing</u>

Write a letter that will be read in a radio broadcast. In your letter, state your position on the hazards or benefits of video games. Try to convince the listening audience to agree with you by using detailed and convincing information.

27. <u>Writing Situation</u>

Drinking and driving can have dangerous consequences. The state government is now considering legislation which would bar teens from driving once they are convicted of Driving Under the Influence (DUI). Should teens who are caught drinking and driving lose their licenses until they are 21, or should the courts give them another chance before they lose their licenses?

<u>Directions for Writing</u>

Write a letter to your state congressional representative. Explain whether you support or oppose a law requiring teens to give up their licenses if they are convicted of DUI. Include reasons and evidence to convince your representative to support your position.

28. <u>Writing Situation</u>

Students from kindergarten to college must take tests frequently in their classes to pass grade levels or to graduate from school. Recently, your state has proposed legislation which would require all students to pass a test every year in order to be promoted to the next grade. Are these high-stakes tests necessary in school, or should these kinds of tests be eliminated in schools? What do you think?

<u>Directions for Writing</u>

Write an essay which you would publish on a Web-based message board for the PTA. Appeal to your audience by explaining your views on the proposed high-stakes testing system. Try to persuade readers of your essay to agree with you by providing well-developed supporting arguments.

29. <u>Writing Situation</u>

The first amendment to the United States of America Constitution states that "Congress shall make no law respecting an establishment of religion or prohibiting the free exercise thereof . . ." Based on this amendment, some people believe that prayer should be permitted in public schools. Others feel that praying violates the principle of separation of the church and the state. The governor and state legislature are about to make decisions about this issue. As a student, you will be affected by their decisions. What is your opinion about students praying in public schools?

<u>Directions for Writing</u>

Write a letter to the governor explaining whether you agree or disagree with allowing prayer in the public schools. Use clear reasons and examples to try to convince the governor to agree with your position.

30. <u>Writing Situation</u>

Your health teacher has been discussing how the environment in which children grow up is very important to their development. Your class has discussed the positives and negatives of life in the city, rural areas, and the suburbs. Which place do you think is a better environment for raising children?

<u>Directions for Writing</u>

Write an essay that you will read in class discussing the positive aspects of raising children in the city, rural areas, or the suburbs. Give convincing reasons and clear examples that support your opinion.

Copyright © American Book Company

APPENDIX B: WRITING RESOURCES

WEB SITES

NOTE: As you may already have experienced, Web sites tend to disappear or even change in form and intent. American Book Company only suggests these sites; it is not responsible for any changes that the sites may incur.

These Web sites include a variety of information with links to still more sites designed as supplemental aids for students. We visited these sites and devised a rating system for them.

Ratings:

Excellent	✎✎✎✎
Good	✎✎✎
Fair	✎✎
Poor	✎

Ask Miss Grammar

For this site, first, you must ignore the silly, stereotypical cartoon lady. Then, and only then, does this Web site have a lot going for it. There is an option to look through "archives," where you select an item you wish to learn more about, bring up facts and games, or you could choose the option to e-mail a specific question to the site. The site states that it cannot answer all e-mails, but it tries to answer many of them. There is an option (found by clicking on Readers' Questions) where you may hear and compare recordings of "God Save the Queen" and "My Country 'Tis of Thee." That particular page is titled American and British English.

Web address   http://www.protrainco.com/grammar.htm   Rating - ✎✎✎

ESL Home Page

The ESL Home Page is a great starting place for ESOL and ESL students working on the Web. It contains many links to the areas of study that any student requires help in, as well as having a site for jobs and for ESL chat rooms. The best features are the grammar and writing games and activities which can be found here. We were unable to visit every site linked to this home page, so choose your links carefully. Some possibilities are links on the left-hand side about writing, grammar, idioms, and more.

Web address   http://www.rong-chang.com/   Rating - ✎✎✎

Caroline's ESL Web Site

Emphasizing grammar and logic, this site offers interactive quizzes and simple self-study lessons. While designed for ESL students, the exercises may be helpful for remedial practice for native English speakers as well. The Hangman game (under the "Games" link) is a fun way to hone vocabulary and spelling skills for simple adjectives. Also try the self-study quizzes.

Web address   http://members.aol.com/Ccochran50/novaesl.htm   Rating - ✎✎✎

Copyright © American Book Company

Interesting Things for ESL Students

While the site is designed for ESL students, native English speakers may use its many activities to sharpen English skills as well. The site is filled with a variety of quizzes, word games, word puzzles, anagrams, lessons, and a random-sentence generator. The interactive pages are marked with a code to indicate whether they require Flash, Java or Javascript technology, and links are included to the free download sites for the software required.

Web address   http://www.manythings.org   Rating - 🖊🖊🖊

Paradigm: Online Writing Assistant

This site features long discussions on how to write essays and some tips on revising and editing work. Clearly written and organized, this is a good source for those who want a review of the composition process.

Web address   http://www.powa.org/   Rating - 🖊🖊🖊

BOOKS AND SOFTWARE

This section contains a listing of books which provide students with grammar and writing instruction in various formats.

Basics Made Easy: Grammar and Usage Review

This book provides clear explanations and plentiful practice exercises on grammar, punctuation, and usage. Chapter reviews reinforce concepts taught in each lesson. The book is a thorough and excellent support for aspiring writers.

Pintozzi, Frank, and Devin Pintozzi. *Basics Made Easy: Grammar and Usage Review*. Woodstock, GA: American Book Co., 1998, revised 2007.
Web address   www.americanbookcompany.com

Basics Made Easy: Grammar and Usage Software

This interactive software program offers a comprehensive review for grammar, punctuation, and usage. Exercises require students to choose the best answers. The software tracks students' scores and correlates with lessons in the companion text, *Basics Made Easy: Grammar and Usage Review* (American Book Company).

Pintozzi, Frank, and Devin Pintozzi. *Basics Made Easy: Grammar and Usage Software*. Woodstock, GA: American Book Co., 2000.
Web address   www.americanbookcompany.com

Copyright © American Book Company

Focus: From Paragraph to Essay

The author, Martha E. Campbell, presents a practical and easy-to-read text that integrates composition and grammar concepts. She includes plentiful exercises, assorted writing topics, and extensive examples of student writing.

Campbell, Martha E. *Focus: From Paragraph to Essay.* Upper Saddle River, NJ: Prentice Hall, 1996.

Writer's Choice: Grammar and Composition

This hard-back text contains lessons in composition, grammar, resources, and literature. The composition activities are particularly helpful for improving writing skills.

Royster, Jacqueline Jones, et al. *Writer's Choice: Grammar and Composition.* New York: McGraw-Hill, 1996.

A Writer's Guide to Transitional Words and Expressions

This book is a helpful companion reference to *A Writer's Guide to Using Eight Methods of Transition* (see below). It contains over 1000 transitional words and expressions that will make your writing effective, logical, and easier to read.

Pellegrino, Victor C. *A Writer's Guide to Transitional Words and Expressions.* Wailuku, HW: Maui Arthoughts, 1987.

A Writer's Guide to Using Eight Methods of Transition

A brief but excellent guide, this book is an invaluable reference tool that helps writers choose the best transitional words and expressions for a context. The author, Victor C. Pellegrino, provides many examples of how to create effective transitions and connections in sentences and paragraphs.

Pellegrino, Victor C. *A Writer's Guide to Using Eight Methods of Transition.* Wailuku, HI: Maui Arthoughts, 1987.

Writing From A to Z: The Easy-to-Use Reference Handbook

This book is organized alphabetically like a dictionary. Consequently, students can easily find, for example, an explanation of a "paragraph" by looking in the letter "P"section. The book covers a wide range of grammar and usage information.

Ebest, Sally Barr. *Writing From A to Z: The Easy-to-Use Reference Handbook.* Mountain View, CA: Mayfield, 1997.

Writing Talk: Sentences and Paragraphs with Readings

A workbook that is too good to be a workbook, *Writing Talk* is worth its weight in good grades for its readings alone. It also has a thorough review of basic concepts and instruction written with wit and an understanding of how to build the skill of writing.

Winkler, Anthony C. and Jo Ray McCuen-Metherell. *Writing Talk: Sentences and Paragraphs with Readings*. 3rd ed. Upper Saddle River, NJ: Prentice Hall, 2003.

Writing Talk: Paragraphs and Short Essays with Readings

This is the second volume of the *Writing Talk* book series. See above for comments.

Winkler, Anthony C. and Jo Ray McCuen-Metherell. *Writing Talk: Sentences and Paragraphs with Readings*. 3rd ed. Upper Saddle River, NJ: Prentice Hall, 2003.

The Young Person's Guide to Becoming a Writer

Reading this book will be a different experience than reading the others. This particular guide is gently encouraging to those students who want to pursue a career in writing but are not sure how to take the first steps. There are sections on improving writing skills, understanding literary genres, and keeping a writer's notebook. This is a first look into the world of professional writing, and it is good for everyone to know the ways to enter that world.

Grant, Janet E. *The Young Person's Guide to Becoming a Writer*. Minneapolis: Free Spirit, 1995.

Copyright © American Book Company